28 Biblioteca d'Arte **Skira**

Paolo Brogini
Mario Di Salvo

An Analysis of Pre-Columbian Sellos of Ecuador

with Special Reference to Anthropomorphic Iconography

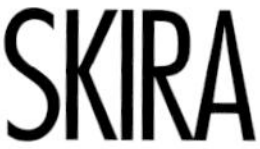

Design
Marcello Francone

Editorial Coordination
Eva Vanzella

Editing
Emily Ligniti

Layout
Marina Boer

Translation
Aldo Matteucci

Translation Coordinator
Carolyn Gossage

Photo Credits
ALEPH, Como (I)
Gabriele Rovelli
Ugo Ambroggio

First published in Italy
in 2011 by
Skira editore S.p.A.
Palazzo Casati Stampa
via Torino 61
20123 Milano
Italy
www.skira.net

Printed and bound in Italy.
First edition

The authors are deeply
grateful to Thomas B.F.
Cummins for his foreword.
For giving encouragement
for this study and for valuable
suggestions the authors want
to thank especially Francis
Cousin, Carolyn Gossage,
Albert Jornet, Margrit
Markstaller, Aldo Matteucci,
Robin Skeates.

Table of Contents

Foreword

The coast of Ecuador is one of the world's great "cradles of civilization". Composed of a rich alluvial plain with a tropical climate, the coast offered its earliest inhabitants both a rich marine life as well as wonderful opportunities first for hunting and gathering and then sedentary farming. It is also one of the earliest places in the Americas where ceramics appeared amongst the culture known as Valdivia, between circa 3200 and 1000 BC. This achievement, in and of itself, tells us just a little of Ecuador's pivotal importance in terms of artistic and technological development in world history. But if we look at the kinds of works that were produced over the thousands of years before the European arrival, we find an astonishing array of truly beautiful and intricate works that can be called art, things that were created by the peoples of Ecuador that had no base or utilitarian function but were finely crafted objects that were produced to please both Mankind and their Cosmos. Ranging from gold, platinum and silver figurines and body adornments to textiles, the coast of Ecuador was a place where artisans, male and female, developed traditions in architecture, metallurgy, weaving and ceramics. The complex technologies of metalworking and ceramic production that were handed down over generations eventually spread throughout the Americas, from Peru in the south and to Mexico in the north. For example the use of molds for making ceramic figurines first appeared in Ecuador by around 1000 BC and later became important in the great ceramic tradition of the Moche (1–600 AD) on the dry coast of Peru. On the other hand, metalwork in gold, silver and tin spread from the coast of Ecuador to the west coast of Mexico around 900 AD.

These archaeological facts are rarely taken into account when the histories of the great Pre-Columbian cultures are recounted in modern books. Rather, we read about the Aztecs and the Incas and their local ancestors as being the Promethean cultures that produced the artistic marvels that the Europeans encountered and described. In fact, Pizzaro and his men quickly moved from the tropical coast of modern day Ecuador down the Pacific coast as it became increasing drier, in search of the Inca and their already fabled wealth. They had, however, encountered off the Ecuadorian coast merchants aboard a seagoing raft that was laden with textiles, ceramics and objects of gold. But this encounter was quickly forgotten as the ransom for the Inca king, Atahualpa (a room filled with gold), began to be shipped back to Europe. Nonetheless, archaeology of the last two centuries as well as *huaqueros* (grave robbers) have revealed the wealth of artistic and technological innovation that mark Ecuador as a generative place.

So, it is an important task that Paolo Brogini and Mario Di Salvo have undertaken in bringing to light one of the oldest and most enduring genres of ceramics in Ecuador: the *sello* or seal. Interesting the hypothesis of the authors relating to the use of *sellos*: *sellos* as a form of communication and *sellos* as amulets or ritual objects. We have only the vaguest idea of how the earliest seals were used in Ecuador; however, the seal is in general a truly interesting object as it is the permanent mirror trace of an image that was transferred to another, more ephemeral surface, be it the human body or woven cloth. At the same time the seal is often more than a mere device for the transference of an image. It can also be regarded as the manifestation of whatever that images means, or better said, the *sello* stands in place of what is absent. For example, in Western Medieval and Renaissance culture, a seal was the presence of the absent emperor and it would be conducted into a town borne aloft a horse on a saddle of velvet, with streets lined with citizens awaiting its entrance as if it were the monarch himself. There is also evidence that the seal as well as the ceramic mold had a similar importance and the possession of the seal (and the mold) was an important emblem of social and/or political importance.

Ceramic molds first appear in Ecuador around 1500 BC and are among the first seals created in the Americas. Moreover, they continued to be used by Ecuadorian Pre-Columbian cultures throughout the following 2000 years. In fact, the importance of the seal continued into the colonial period and is recorded in use among indigenous cultures on the coast in the twentieth century. Ecuadorian seals may not have been so revered as representing the person of the Pre-Columbian ruler in one of the coastal cultures of Chorrera, Regional Development, and Manteño as they were in Europe, but they are one of the few symbolic objects that is common to all of the coastal Ecuadorian cultures. With an estimated date of origin around 1500 BC, seals are associated with almost all coastal cultures. As described and illustrated in Paolo Brogini and Mario Di Salvo's marvelous book, the seals not only have a long tradition in Pre-Hispanic coastal Ecuador, but there is a consistency in both form and design. The ceramic seal is almost always made either in the form of a hollow cylinder or as a flat plane. The designs are most often abstract; although the majority illustrated in this book are figural. Most surprisingly the line of the image is often curvilinear as much as it is straight and angled. This implies that the designs do not come only from weaving, a major Andean medium, but are also derived from freehand drawing and painting on surfaces, be they textile, wood or ceramic. That is, one can sense the artist's hand as he makes the soft clay with a stylus of some sort in the same way one can detect the movement of the artist's hand in a drawing.

One of the great pleasures of working with seals is that one can use them in much the same way that ancient Pre-Columbian artists used them, covering the seal with some pigment and then pressing or rolling it on to some other surface. One can find the same experience using ancient molds, pressing soft clay into them and then building a new vessel or figurine much in the same way as the ancient Ecuadorian artists did. This participation in the creative process, shared across millennia, is a great privilege as one learns to manipulate these objects. And it is clear from the illustrations and text of these authors that they have taken great joy and have learned a great deal by studying and using these seals. To underline the scientific importance of the numerous dates that were revealed as a result of thermoluminescence tests. It is their admiration and respect for the past and its beauty that they share with us in the pages that follow.

Thomas B.F. Cummins
Dumbarton Oaks Professor of the History of Pre-Columbian and Colonial Art and Chair of The Department of History of Art and Architecture - Harvard University - Sackler Museum

Introduction

Art does not show the visible.
It visualises, however, what often might not be.
Paul Klee

The historical events that brought about the thorough fragmentation – if not total eradication – of Pre-Columbian civilisations severed irremediably the chain of knowledge by which meanings and communications from the past are transmitted to the present. In short, their authentic understanding has been lost. Consequently the current approach to Pre-Columbian art often becomes, from sheer necessity, merely aesthetic. This approach is appropriate when referring to artistic evaluation, but it might – on the other hand – diminish an understanding of their functional aspects and, in the end, sidestep the original purpose and use of these artefacts.

The term "art" needs not be limited to contemplative evaluation, particularly when, within a specific tradition, artistic creativity is expressed in objects of everyday use. Ornamental aspects, though genuine, fall far short of revealing the whole story.

The *sellos* are portrayals and patterns expressed in various forms in accordance with associations which embody themselves through symbols, myths and rituals. "Truth" may thus be attained both directly and intuitively.

The world view of the native peoples stipulates a constant flow of communication between universe and mankind (macro-microcosm) so as to better understand and express the various levels that constitute the "truth."[1] The world revealed by the many graphic symbols of Pre-Columbian art is, therefore, deeply fascinating, even though, at first glance, one experiences a sense of impenetrable mystery. For they are the expression of long lost thoughts and vanished truths – symbols that are on the verge of becoming eternally silent.

When we perceive images that show links to the material world, such as forms of humans and animals, we are content to assume that we understand them simply because we recognise them.

But this is merely because we are inclined to find in a work of art only that which is already within our own spiritual consciousness. This is less likely to occur when we encounter abstract stylistic elements. To help in deciphering their meaning we should first delineate the world view and man's role in it as it exists in any culture that has deep roots in the past. No traditional artistic expression has accidental or arbitrary value, much less a personal one. Throughout space and time, mankind has felt – and still feels today – the need to reconcile the real and the invisible world. This need often translates into a tangible and symbolic shape that has its starting point in myths pertaining to origin and initiation rites: matters that modern culture tends to write off as "superstition" . . .

Part I

**Pre-Columbian *Sellos*, with Particular Reference
to those from Ecuador**
Bibliographies and exhibitions of private and public collections
notwithstanding, there remain many unanswered questions with
regard to Pre-Columbian *sellos*. Large numbers have been dis-
covered in numerous Pre-Columbian civilizations, for it is obvious that usages and customs – including the use of *sellos* – have
travelled from one culture to another, moving across the land bridge
constituted by the cultures of Central America all the way to certain regions of Colombia and the coastal regions of Ecuador. Discoveries of *sellos* dating back to the Pre-Columbian cultures of Peru are rare.

In fact, to date, archaeologists and researchers have paid scant
attention to *sellos*. One might even argue that these finds are being ignored despite their wide distribution and abundance. This
lack of much-deserved attention is puzzling, especially since our
knowledge of the history of the people who inhabited the American continent prior to the Spanish conquest rests nearly exclusively on archaeological sources and on the surviving iconography.
Together they constitute almost the sole authentic documentation
relating to *sellos* and therefore remain the only source of available
knowledge.

Among the 600 archaeological findings of Mayan culture on
display at the 1998 Palazzo Grassi exhibition in Venice seven were
sellos. The 700-page catalogue, which represents an immense and
up-to-date source of knowledge on Mayan culture, describes them
as follows: "Smooth monochrome solid ceramic stamps: one side
shows graven drawings and some perforations; two of them exhibit anthropomorphic figures. The provenance of these stamps
is identified as a centre of large-scale clay production."[2] There is,
however, a notable absence of any sort of description on the use
of the objects in question.

In 2004, five *sellos* were part of an exhibition in Rome, at
Palazzo Ruspoli, devoted to the Aztec culture.[3] At the 1975 exhi-

bition on the art of Colombia at the Petit Palais in Paris, a total of seven *sellos* were displayed among the Pre-Columbian finds.[4] The fact might be worth mentioning that at the important exhibition on Pre-Hispanic cultures of Peru that took place at Palazzo Strozzi in Florence in 2003, not one *sello* was to be found among the more than 300 archaeological artefacts on view. Nor is there any mention whatsoever made of such objects in the critical catalogue of the exhibition, despite the fact that over 300 pages are devoted to a rich and articulated overview of the ancient civilizations of this Andean country.[5] It is a notable absence that serves as confirmation of the limited number of *sellos* recovered in Peru compared to geographic areas to the north, starting with Ecuador.

Sellos from Peru are mentioned in the works of John Alden Mason[6] and Alan Lapiner. The latter describes a flat *sello* as follows: "Ceramic seal (stamp) with aviary glyph", and another cylindrical *sello* as: "Cylinder seal (stamp) feline and interlocking serpent motifs".[7] In his in-depth monograph dating back to 1958, José Alcina Franch writes: *"Las 'Pintaderas' mejicanas y sus relaciones"*, referring to his own quantitative survey on the geographic distribution of the *sellos* in Central America, Antilles and South American areas and mentions only one *sello* from the Peru (northern coast), now in the collection of the Berliner Museum für Völkerkunde.[8]

At the regional level, in Ecuador all the *sellos* found thus far are made of baked clay and belong only to coastal populations. They also pertain specifically to a number of cultures that have developed there.[9] All *sellos* shown and described in this study are exclusively archaeological finds from Ecuadorian cultures. The great majority of them may be attributed to two cultures in particular: Jama-Coaque and Manteña.

Several important exhibitions were organized in the past on the ancient civilizations of Ecuador. Among the most representative ones in Europe one may cite the rich and vast overview that took place in Venice in 1982 at Palazzo Grassi. The exhibition covered 6000 years of civilisation under the evocative title of *The Treasures of the Earth of Atahualpa. Ecuador from its prehistory until the Incas.*

Attention was drawn to the *sellos* on this occasion: they were reproduced in the catalogue and described as "seals" made of terracotta.[10] The same exhibition was later presented in Switzerland in 1982 at the Castello Visconteo in Locarno.

Worldwide, arguably the most important exhibition of *sellos* from Ecuador took place at Guayaquil in 1996. The exhibition displayed over 200 *sellos* chosen with great care from among approximately 1,200 in the collections of the Museo Antropológico of the Banco Central de Guayaquil. The related catalogue[11] remains today one of the best sources of up-to-date information and knowledge. The underlying basis for their selection was that they all belonged to the coastal culture called Jama-Coaque (300/200 BC–700 AD) and explains the title selected for the exhibition, *Los sellos de Jama-Coaque*.

Archaeological areas

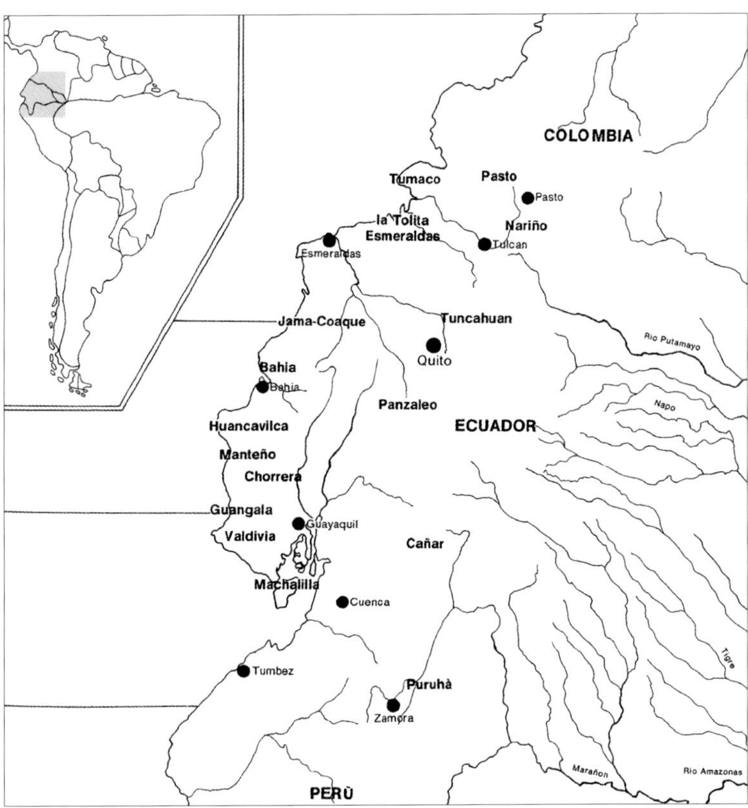

Sellos and Seals

Though similar in shape, *sellos* distinguish themselves markedly from seals like those which originated in the Middle East as early as the fifth millennium BC[12]: they differ in the materials used for their manufacture as well as their intended use. Middle Eastern seals were usually made of stone, often precious ones, in which the negative of an image had been carved. On affixing the seal it would leave in a soft material (clay, wax, lacquer, etc.) a positive imprint of a figure representing a person, property or control. With only extremely rare exceptions, *sellos* are shaped or carved in clay so that the resulting image corresponds to the design on their surface (carving as positive). It is therefore inappropriate to qualify the Ecuadorian *sellos* as seals, and this applies as well to those Pre-Columbian *sellos* that have been identified throughout the meso-American region and the northern Andean area beginning with the second millennium BC.[13]

Sellos come in two basic shapes. One is flat and distinguished by a cone-shaped handle at the back for ease of handling.[14] The other has a cylindrical shape, and may or may not be pierced along the central axis. The purpose of the two types of *sellos* is thus substantially different. With regard to the flat ones, the pattern is essentially complete and self-contained, while with a cylindrical surface the pattern is repeated time and again when it is rolled over the surface. Furthermore, the dimensions of a flat *sello*, even when extremely small,[15] seem to be related to their use. The same can be said about the size of cylindrical *sellos*.[16] Most of them are between 6 and 7 cm long with an average circumference of between 3 and 4 cm.

Intended Uses of *Sellos*

The more common hypothesis considers *sellos* to be matrices and their intended use for the decoration of body or textiles.

The catalogue of the exhibition devoted to the art of Colombia held in Paris at the Petit Palais in 1975 already stated that a *sello* "served to decorate the body or to stamp cotton tissues."[17]

In the catalogue for the 2004 exhibition devoted to the Aztec culture in Rome at Palazzo Ruspoli, *sellos* were described as "stamps": "In the Aztec culture, the stamps' popularity derived from a taste for colours and patterns to be applied to dresses and body. The surface on which the paint was applied determined the shape of the stamp: we have cylindrical stamps for printing continuous patterns, mainly cloth and dresses; convex ones were used to paint thighs and arms; or they might be used for decorating pottery prior to firing; flat stamps were used on textiles . . . The application of patterns using such objects took on, if possible, the character of rituals that were performed in ceremonies and for special events, even though the use of body paint was probably a daily occurrence."[18] Unfortunately such pronouncements are not supported by archaeological evidence from textiles that would bear patterns stamped on them by means of *sellos*, or from objects decorated by the method described in the catalogue.

The relatively brief catalogue published on the occasion of the exhibition *The Treasures of the Land of Atahualpa. Ecuador from its prehistory until the Incas* at the Castello Visconteo in Locarno in 1982 turns out to be an important source of documentation for *sellos*. Referring to those on view it defines them as *pintaderas*[19] and describes them as follows: "They are a type of seal, cylindrical or flat in shape, and they were used to paint textiles or to create tattoos on the human body using geometric or fantasy patterns."[20] In fact, in the sixteenth century, Brother Diego de Landa, in his chronicle of the conquest of Mexico, uses the term *pintaderas* to identify the instrument with which ancient Mexicans printed lively colours and patterns on the body.[21]

Referring to flat *sellos* Ms Parducci asserts: "*Sello o pintadera es un instrumento mecánico cuya función es estampar dibujos en el cuerpo, tejidos, etc. La pintura corporal tuvo por finalidad, más que por uso decorativo, una función ritual o mágico-religiosa. Se pintaban el cuerpo para ceremonias religiosas, danzas sagradas, guerra, caza y otros. Posiblemente los temas de decoración corporal debían ser motivos característicos apropiados, a los actos a representar en su tribu.*"[22]

The chapter in the catalogue of the exhibition at the Museo Antropológico of the Banco Central de Guayaquil in 1996 begins therefore by describing as follows the intended use of *sellos*[23]: "*Todavia no existen evidencias directas que nos indiquen para qué fueron usados los sellos...*" It rejects with robust arguments the hypothesis that the same *sellos* were used for applications on cotton fabric, this being the most recurrent hypothesis in the literature, perhaps influenced by the wide distribution of traditional methods of manual printing using positive stamps. In such a paradigm, colouring would have been applied to the stamp surface and then pressed onto the textile. After each application colouring would be applied anew to the surface. In order for the pattern to stay fast after washing, the textile material would need to be treated with appropriate mordents. It is doubtful that such chemicals were known at the time. Most likely Pre-Columbian textiles were woven from agave (sisal) fibres, which poorly absorb colour. Cotton was only introduced in much more recent times. All this tends to undermine the hypothesis that *sellos* were used as stamps for textiles.[24] This is further substantiated by the fact that some *sellos*, though provided with a handle, show a plane-convex configuration that is at odds with its possible use for printing on tissue.

Equivalent arguments hold for cylindrical *sellos*. There the pigment which is applied to the rolling surface would need replenishing after each rotation or the colour would be applied unevenly. After each new pigment application, it is difficult to maintain perfect continuity of the imprint, unless one supposes – but it seems an absurdity – a second cylinder which applies the colour to the external surface of the *sello* and its pattern as it rotates simultaneously. According to D'Harcourt: "Up to the present I have formed no definite conclusion as to whether or not the Peruvians made use of incised stamps to impress the painted design on the surface of fabric. In all the specimens I have examined where the same motif is used as a decorative theme, I have found that there is variation in the dimensions of the motif and in the arrangement of its parts, and that such variation cannot be attributed to the distortion of the fabric."[25]

A much more plausible hypothesis is that flat *sellos* might have been used in the context of religious ceremonies to apply colouring to the human body.[26] Even when limited to its most probable use, this conjecture still fails to explain why such a method of decorating the human body was employed when it would seem more logical to use the simpler and bolder patterns still in use which are typical of the populations that have been using them for centuries.

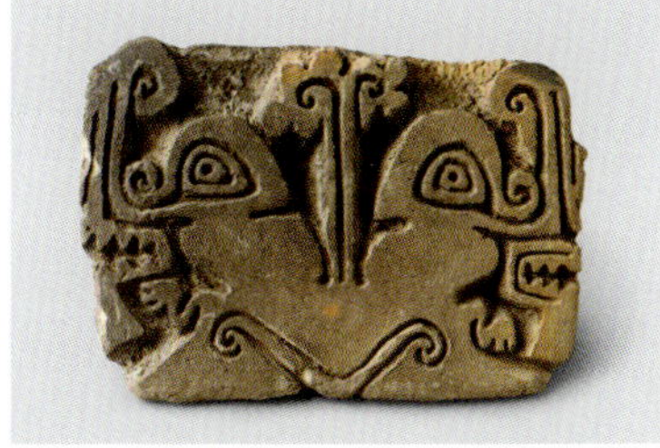
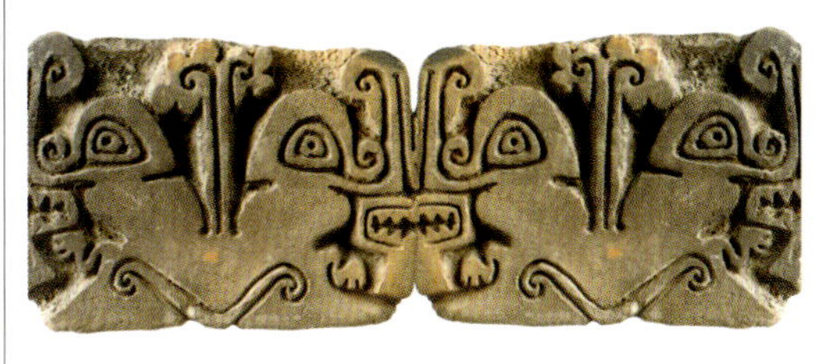

P 40

In the case of more complex or peculiar patterns used for body decorations such an objection might not hold. The flat *sello* **P 40** might be such an instance: it represents anthropo/zoomorphic images where the human mask emerges from placing mirrored zoomorphs next to each other. Placing by stamping next to each other two images of this *sello*, an image emerges hidden under the form of a second mask, which recalls a jaguar.

In this way it is possible to observe images consisting of different patterns, which blend into each other and fascinate the viewer in characteristic ways. It is the ambivalence of twofold images with enigmatic meanings which are concealed under hidden images. Such an elegant drawing could only be realised by stamping it with a *sello*, but certainly not with other instruments or decorative means.

One might also point to the interesting research of Anthony Oregon, which was published in the United States in 1999. Oregon suggests that *sellos* might have been used to decorate food and bread in particular.[27] This tradition is still alive in many countries today. On the other hand, given the positive imaging typical of *sellos*, the possibility that such imprinting may also have been used on wet sand or soft material such as clay remains doubtful.

Occasionally other functions have also been considered such as stamping on ceramics, or paper (papyrus) and animal skins; identification of people and objects, issue of free passage, ownership certification, value of exchange, message authentication; and lastly as decorative elements in chains – this would apply especially to cylindrical *sellos* which are axially perforated or grooved across both ends.

In conclusion, one might add that any repeated use of *sellos* – as in printing – would inevitably lead to wear and tear and eventual disposal when the *sello* was no longer fit for its intended use.

Iconography

It is possible to distinguish different kinds of iconographies on *sellos*: anthropo/zoo/phytomorphic (at times highly stylised) and geometric. Perhaps one might also consider a hieroglyphic function. As already mentioned, the images in numerous *sellos* are often immediately recognizable. Other images belong to a world of symbols and myths which is expressed and translated in almost ciphered language whose interpretative key has been lost; they might contain cryptic allusions that puzzle as well as fascinate and lead researchers to suggest interpretations on purely intuitive grounds. Thus, in describing a *sello*,[28] Klein and Cevallos write: "Geometric images composed of symbols, these stamps keep secrets in their labyrinthine calligraphy: memories of deeds, bands, sacred representations".[29]

Other *sellos* have been created as double images in which one might see alternative portraits. A special power of fascination attaches to this double identity in which one image transforms itself into the other. This troubling visualisation may happen at first glance, or only after protracted observation. Image within image, shapes that emerge depending on the state of mind of the observer, a sense of mystery grounded or merely hinted at in the ambivalence of these double features. A mystical phenomenon of multiple images and of enigmatic representation is employed, in which the image is hidden behind the veil of a theme: this reveals a heightened sensitivity among the people in question for disguised images, whether real or imaginary. Both flat as well as cylindrical *sellos* of Ecuadorian cultures feature not only double but apparently also triple, if not quadruple, images. This idiosyncrasy would seem to be specific to these cultures, especially Jama-Coaque, and would in itself merit in-depth and specific study.[30]

Symbolic Value of *Sellos*
Sellos as a Form of Communication

"Archaic and traditional people essentially used symbols in written communications, thus establishing permanent relationships between sign and the symbolised object. Their knowledge is expressed symbolically because their sacred symbols manifest in real and authentic ways the energies that they represent, and in which they mediate. The magic in the symbol rests on the analogy that links it enduringly to what it symbolises, and identifies itself with it."[31] The iconographies in Pre-Columbian *sellos* might therefore represent elements of communication deserving study from various points of view.

Giuseppe Ricchieri, a missionary of the Combonian religious order who was active in Ecuador for forty years, has written: "With regard to the Ecuadorian area we might consider the 'seals' as a means of communication used in the period spanning 1800 BC to 1500 AD. A complete message might have been recorded on terracotta tablets of composite character. Perforated cylindrical seals might be slipped in succession onto a string to create a message."[32] New horizons might be opened by discoveries substantiating this conjecture.

This would be particularly welcome for the Andean cultures which, contrary to meso-American cultures, have left no trace of writing. "A pattern, often complex and highly articulated, might have been a more congenial means of communication to the Andean tradition"[33] for it substantiated "the graphic technique to be a better tool than alphabetic writing in explaining certain religious and philosophical concepts."[34]

Surely Pre-Columbian *sellos* were, among their other possible functions, also a widely distributed instrument for the transmission of symbols by means of images and signs: "*En todo caso el hecho de llevar estas tabletas o sellos, tanto en Ecuador como en otros paises, un significado ritual o religioso, demuestra el comienzo de la asociación de figuras graficadas, relacionadas con pensamientos determinados, o sea el primer paso hacia la constitución del sistema de glifos, y por lo tanto de una escritura embrionaria.*"[35] This being said, one must remember that writing evolved in the same way in all cultures, namely with representations of images and thoughts through the use of progressively more abstract pictograms.

Communication – an exercise in *pars pro toto* – implies a distance between the agent and the recipient of the communication: face to face communication needs no object for mediation. Distance may be diachronic, as when the past is recorded in temples. Gods are distant, and so are the dead. By extension, distance may refer to the future: divination might be seen as anticipatory communication. Communication may refer to geographical distance, and it then is a mnemonic aid over long distances. Communication may refer to societal distance – edicts from the king; or to complexity – records of numerous transactions between merchants.

Sellos as Amulets or Ritual Objects

For obvious lack of evidence the question of the uses of Pre-Columbian *sellos* – be they flat or cylindrical – remains an enigma. Referring to *sellos*, the scholar Frederik v. Field wrote: "In all cases they served a function, and from their quantity, their historical and geographical spread, as well as their artistry, it must have been an important one. But in what did their importance consist? For what were they made? How were they used?"[36]

We find in all cultures apotropaic objects, that is objects with propitiating or talismanic functions and destined to ward off dangers. Lacking other explanations we might venture the hypothesis that in Pre-Columbian cultures *sellos* fulfilled this function. "What we must understand is the fact that a symbol is really an energy-force which truly represents the being or the represented object and not simply their 'allegory'."[37] The sun, the animals, the geometric figures refer back to a reality that constitutes a whole: the symbol / συν βάλλω, as the visible representation of the invisible, reconciles the differences and makes them one (the devil / δια βάλλω is its opposite). "In traditional and primitive societies, in fact, the symbol represents a real sign, or a set of living signs; they are interlaced and are interrelated through their multiple meanings. In such a way they shape a language, or a cipher code, that is both unique and revealing, belonging exclusively to the society in which they manifest themselves."[38]

As an especially interesting example in this context is to mention the flat *sello* **P 51**: it represents two zoomorphic figures facing each other. It might be read both as positive and negative. Impressing the *sello* as positive, an image emerges hidden under the form of a mask, which recalls a jaguar.

From the very beginning, symbolic communication is at the root of the culture of all peoples. "The 'campesino' might have worked and planted his field, but sprouting and growth of the plants

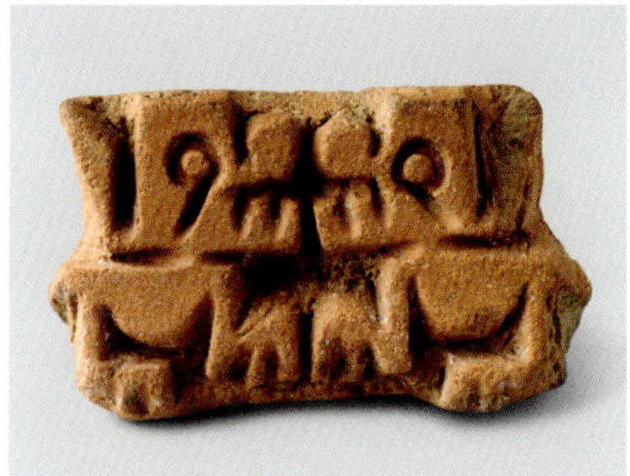

P 51

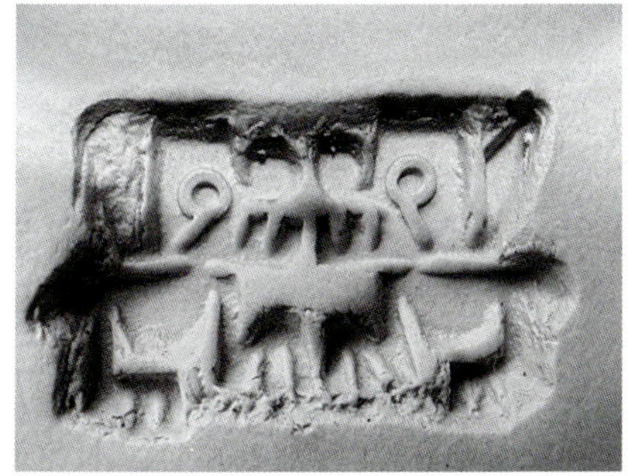

depended on divine intervention. Work was prayer and in order to pray the Indio would sing, dance, cover himself with many-coloured feathers, and paint his face and body. Thus might the images on the *sellos* be read as the translation of the concept of divinity in tangible form . . ."[39]

The fact that many *sellos* have been found perfectly preserved, as if kept in a protective case, and not used until worn out, speaks against a utilitarian function. Presumably they had been kept with great care and "*probablemente enterrados intencionalmente con quien fue su diseño en vida*"[40] as if they were amulets or ritual objects meant to express religious notions and concepts.

Field already lamented the absence of archaeological excavations allowing scientific analysis of the original context in which *sellos* were deposited: "Are *sellos*, for instance, found in all burials, many, or in only a few? In what types of burials are they found, the richer or poorer ones? With what other type of material, figures, pots, or implements are they associated?"[41]

Sellos may also be found in ruins, or middens. Though the odd anecdote may exist, there is no quantitative survey that might link them to any specific kind of site and thus give a possible clue to their function. This imprecision as to the context of their recovery is not helpful in placing them in the context of Pre-Columbian cultures.

John Alden Mason mentions *sellos* placed in Peruvian tombs in his study referring to the inhabitants of the northern coast. Among them: ". . . some stamps recovered in the tombs suggest that they were used to decorate the body with patterns."[42] D'Harcourt also refers to *sellos* recovered in tombs: "*Ainsi, M. Sanchez, ancien propriétaire du lieu, ayant fait exécuter une tranchée dans la partie ouest de la grande tola découvrit à 7 m. à l'intérieur un squelette en position repliée, tenant en main un sceau (pintadera).*"[43] Restrepo also refers to graves: "*La primera característica de ellos es que cada uno contenía sólo un cadáver y junto a éste iban colocadas... pintaderas.*"[44]

All cultures have made use of objects to which mainly – if not exclusively – the function of an amulet was attributed. A vehicle for this function might be – for example – a magical scroll wrapped in a leather sheath, such as those worn around the neck in Ethiopia.

"*Volviendo a los sellos de Manabí*[45] *habría que concluir que los cilíndricos dificilmente hayan sido destinados a impresión, pudiendo admitir ésta finalidad a los sellos planos, sin poder precisar sobre qué material y para qué finalidad. Tal vez los cilindricos hayan sido considerados como adornos, amuletos, señal de distinción o mensajes, y por ende despiertan más la imaginación todavía.*"[46]

Some of the *sellos* – both cylindrical as well as flat – that have been examined appear to have been intentionally divided or broken off along the middle: the proportion is particularly high among the cylindrical *sellos* representing anthropomorphic figures with joined hands or feet.[47]

Could the breakage of the *sellos* be regarded as an example of intentional object fragmentation/sacrifice? Archaeologists have been identifying increasing numbers of examples of this practice in recent years.

Documentary Evidence Relating to the Use of *Sellos*

After encountering a plethora of hypotheses in the process of consulting various publications – including auction catalogues – on Pre-Columbian art generally, and Ecuadorian in particular, further investigation has yielded concrete evidence of a possible function of *sellos*. Several terracotta statues have been found representing human figures with clearly identifiable *sellos* worn singly or in vertical multiples around the neck, or held in the hand.

Di Capua signals one example: "*Es oportuno señalar una figurina de la cultura Jama-Coaque (n° inv. 4-26-79) que exhibe en su mano derecha un sello circular.*"[48] A second example is published by Cummins & Burgos (**fig. 1**). They also point out that: "There are over a hundred female figures wearing a pair of seals in the same position, and some wear a third larger seal hanging like a pendant."[49] No other scholar of Pre-Columbian *sellos* has ever highlighted such evidence in writing. Publishing these images identified as being statues of anthropomorphic figures unquestionably holding *sellos* would therefore appear to be essential. Future comparative studies are likely to yield interesting discoveries. This might be further substantiated by the following further examples: **figs. 1,**[50] **2,**[51] **3.**[52] The **figs. 1–3** figures belongs to the Jama-Coaque culture of the Ecuadorian coast. The three statues portray seated women holding pineapples (*ananas comosus*) or corncobs; their hats are decorated with them (goddess of earth's fertility?). They all wear necklaces with cylindrical *sellos*.

Fig. 4[53] represents a funerary urn pertaining to the Meso-American civilization of the Zapotec, which flourished in the region of Oaxaca on the coast of the Pacific Ocean south of Mexico between 300 BC and the time of the Conquest. Monte Albán was its main centre. The figure represented on the urn wears a hat from which two ears of corn hang at ear level. The statue wears a necklace with a bunch of cylindrical *sellos*.

The Zapotec civilization had been evolving into an independent culture with only limited contacts with the rest of Meso-America, and more intensive ones, it seems, with the Ecuadorian world of the coast, e.g. with the Jama-Coaque culture.[54] The similarities between the three terracotta figures from Jama-Coaque and those of Zapotec represent a sure indication of comparable uses and customs. Further research might pursue this possibility further and yield interesting discoveries.

Figs. 5,[55] **6,**[56] **7,**[57] **8,**[58] **9,**[59] **10,**[60] **11**[61] all portray examples of statues pertaining to the cultures of the Ecuadorian coast (Jama-Coaque and Bahia). Four female figures wear cylindrical *sellos* strung around their necks (**figs. 5, 6, 7, 9**). The other three representing solemn-looking dignitaries – possibly priests or shamans – show cylindrical *sellos* hanging from the neck and one flat held in one hand (**figs. 8, 10, 11**).

The Spanish-*quechua* dictionary (*quechua* is a native language in the Andean area) written in 1608 by Gonçáles Holguin translates the word huaca as: "Idol, little figurines of people and animals that they carry with them"[62] hence portable amulets. If some cylindrical *sellos* were worn as pendants hanging vertically from

1. Seated Female Figure, Jama-Coaque. Around her neck she wears two cylindrical *sellos*. Details of the *sellos*

the neck they must also have had a hole through which a string of vegetable fibre or leather could be threaded. This would explain why many cylindrical *sellos* show a perforation, no matter how small its diameter, and this is further supported by the fact that the rims show little or no wear from use. When cylindrical *sellos* are not perforated the two extremities show indentations that might have been suitable for holding in place a cord or thread.

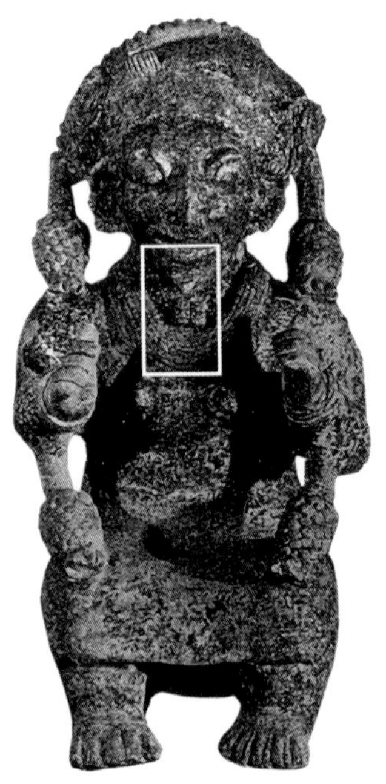

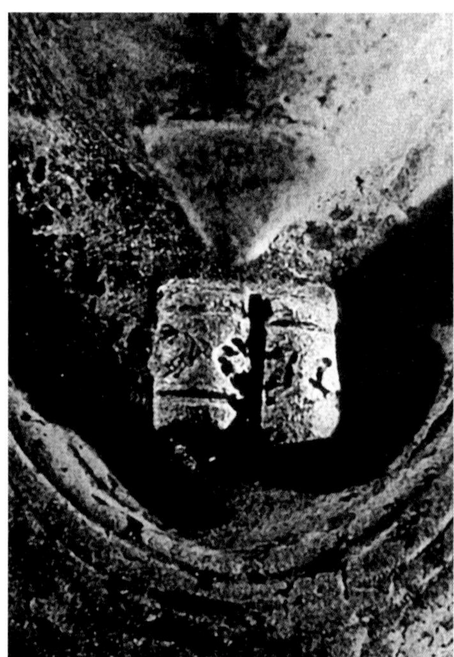

1

2. Pottery, Jama-Coaque, Seated Female Figure. Pineapples (*Ananas comosus*) or corncobs can be seen in her headdress and her hands

3. Seated Female Figure. Brownish pottery. H: 32 cm. Provenance Manabì region

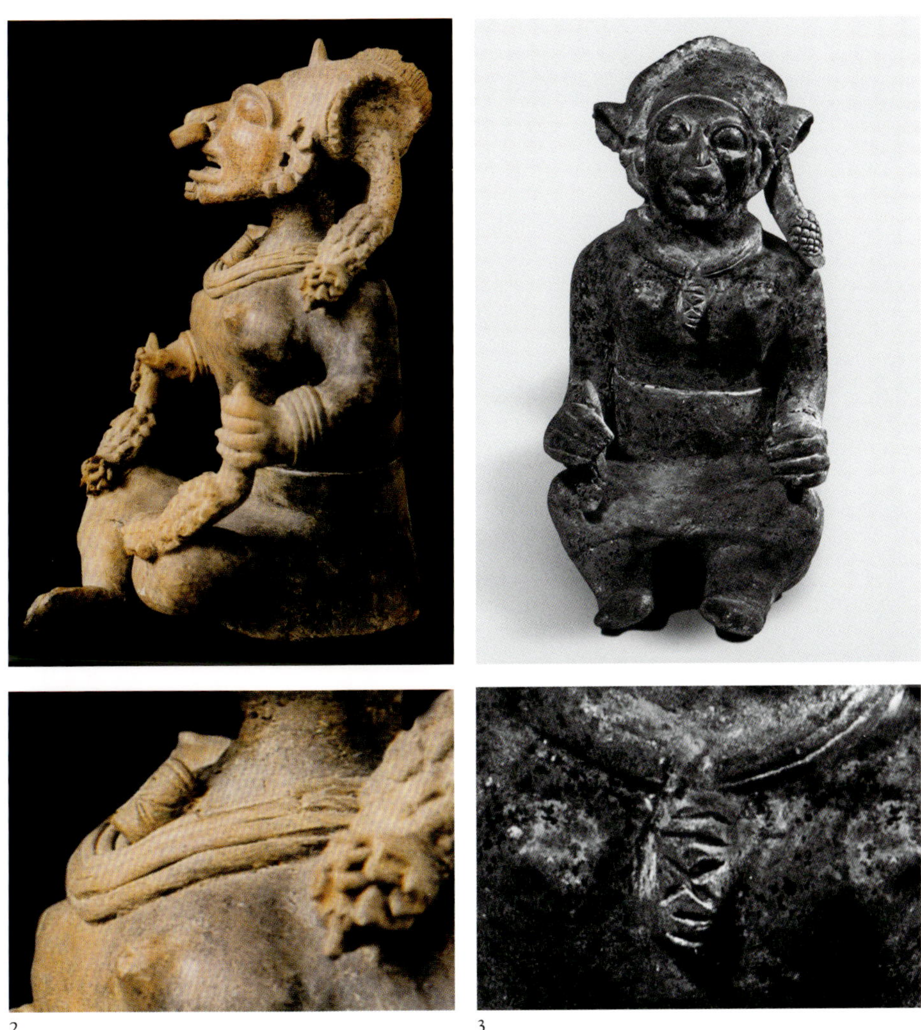

2

3

4. A Zapotec
Figural Urn.
Vienna,
Naturhistorisches
Museum

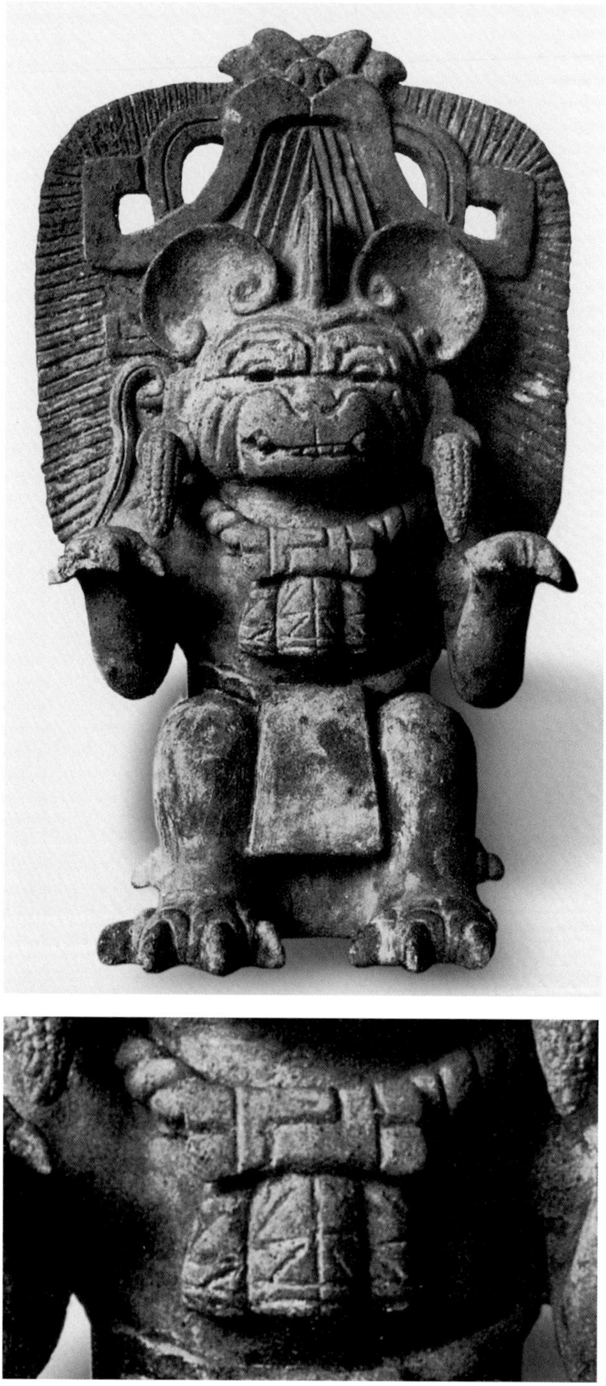

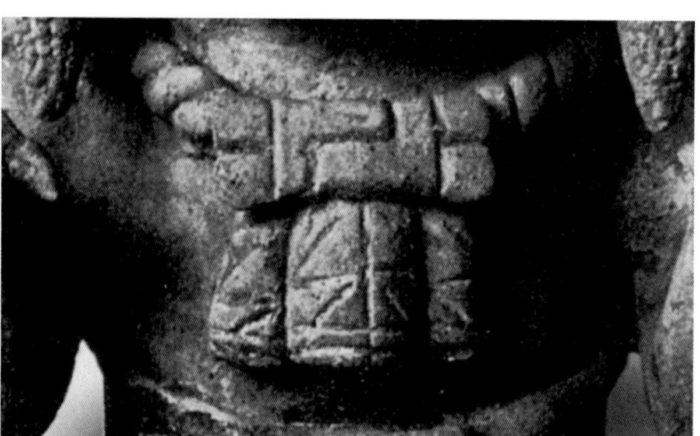

4

5. Pottery, Jama-Coaque, Standing Female Figure. Around the neck she wears one cylindrical *sello*

6. Standing Female Figure. Pottery coloured in gold, turquoise and brown. H: 32 cm. Provenance San Isidoro (Manabì region)

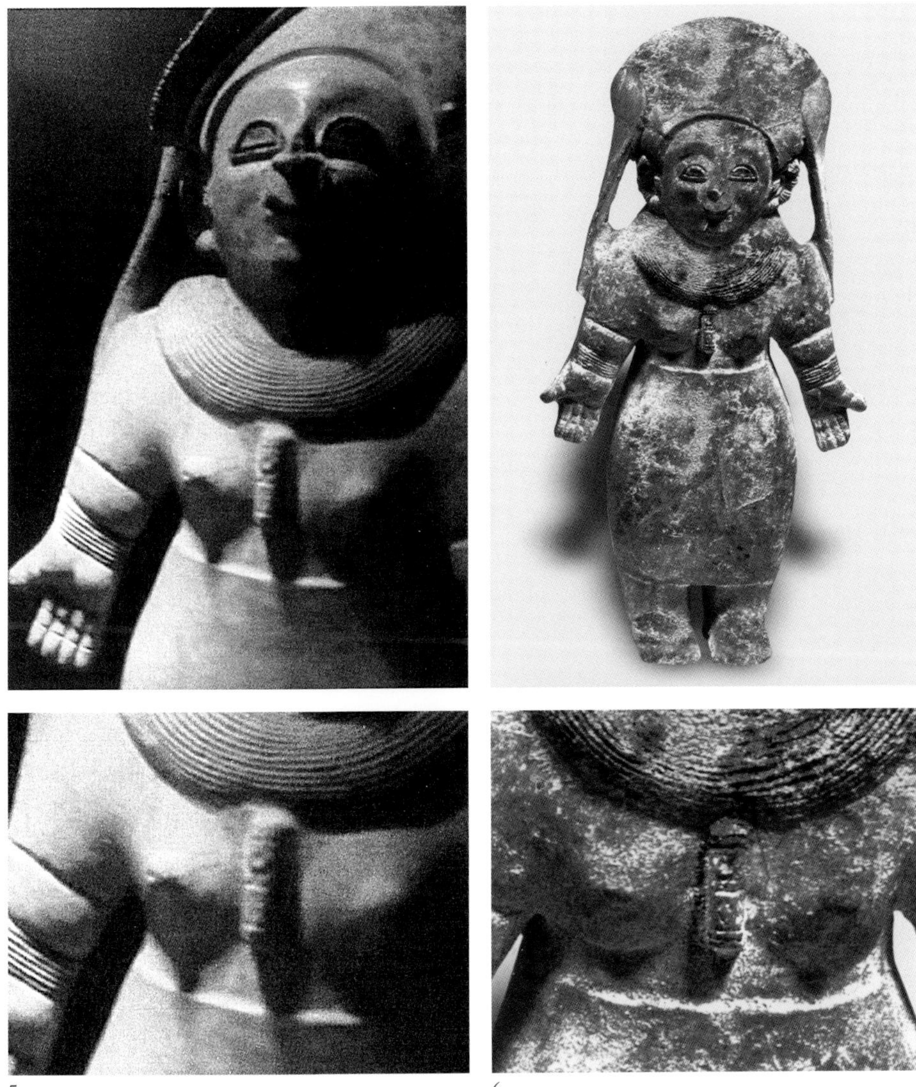

5

6

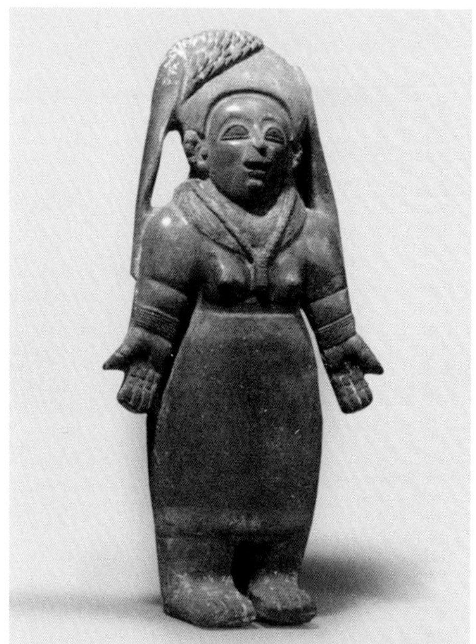

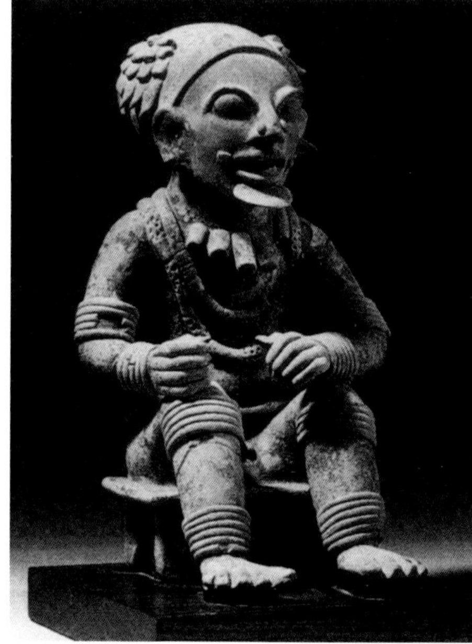

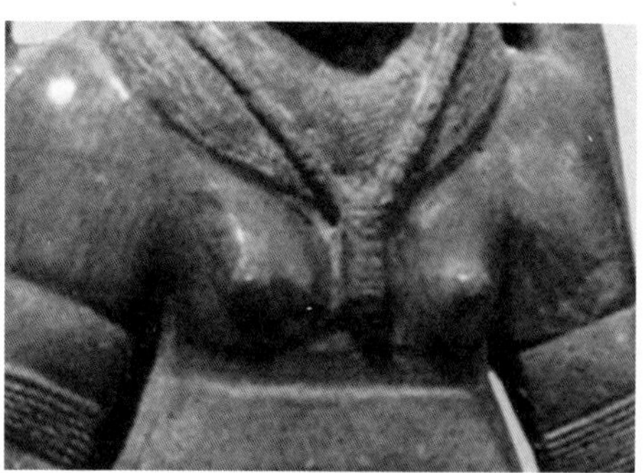

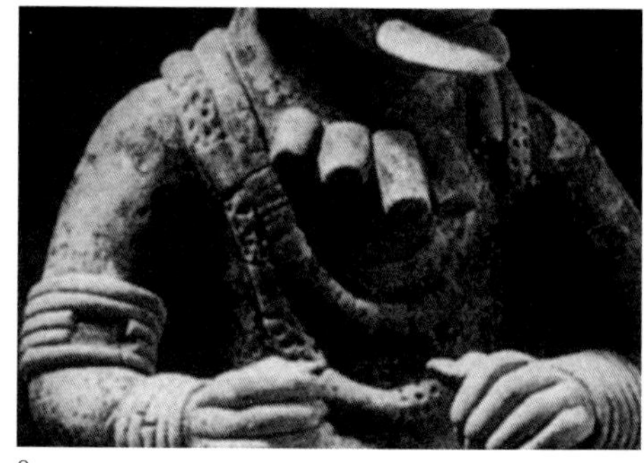

7

8

7. A Manabí Female Figure, Jama-Coaque, 500 BC–500 AD, standing with arms to her side and palms facing forward, adorned with multiple bracelets and collar with overlaid pendant necklage, labret and nose ring, and wearing a long skirt and tufted turban with flaps extending to the shoulder, highlighted with ochre and blue-green pigment. H: 31.1 cm

8. A Jama-Coaque Male Figure, ca. 500 BC–500 AD, the dignitary seated on a four-legged bench with back rounded, the carefully modeled hands cupped and resting on the raised knees, animated face with open mouth and lunate eyes, and the cheeks, chin and nose adorned with labrets and plugs, wearing multiple leg and armbands, strings of shell necklaces, and fleecy turban. H: 26.7 cm

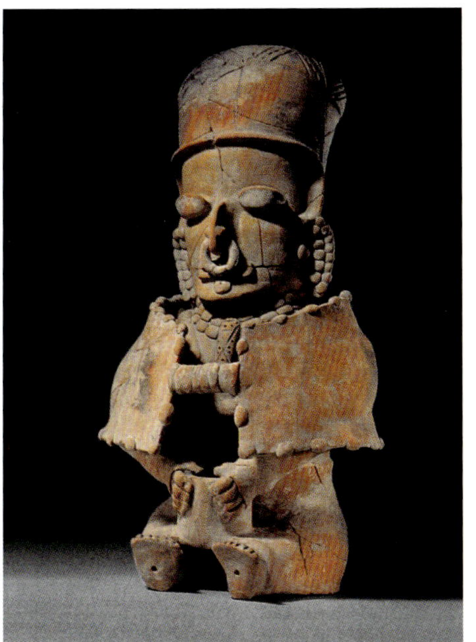

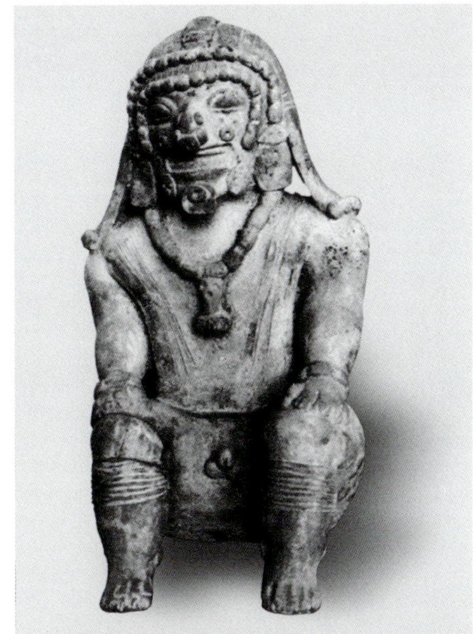

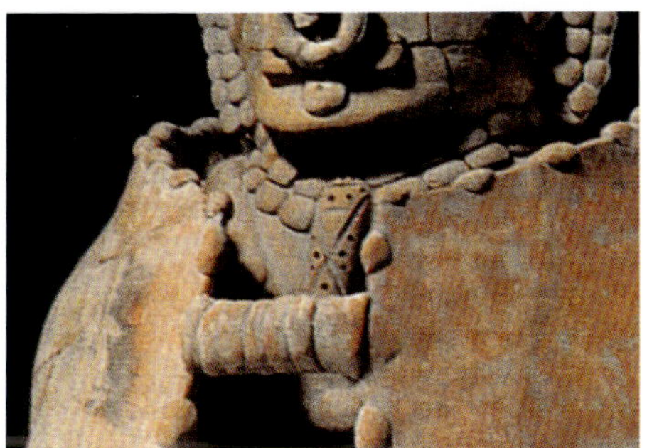

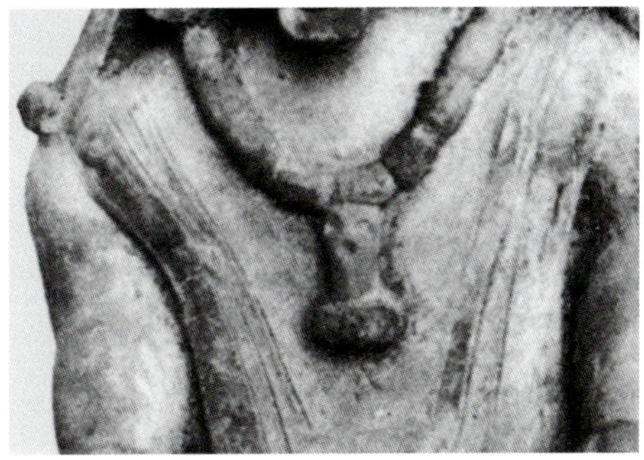

9

10

9. Large Bahia Seated Female Figure, Manabí region, ca. 500 BC–500 AD, with legs extended straight forward and holding a bowl on her lap, the imposing head with lips parted, nose pierced with ring ornament, stylized projecting eyes and ears trimmed by beadwork, wearing a skirt, cape and necklace with shell pendant, the tall close-fitting headdress with patterned band at the top; extensive remains of ochre, red and yellow pigment. H: 64.7 cm

10. Pottery, Jama-Coaque, Seated Male Figure. H: 25 cm; L: 15 cm. Provenance San Isidoro (Manabí region, Inv. no. 2-57-72)

p.32
11. Pottery, Bahia, Seated Shaman. H: 48.5 cm; TLT: - 1800 years. Object description made by the private collector regarding the *sello*: "Esto puede bien representar un sello, pero debido a que la superficie del objeto no ha sido trabajada, no es posible asegurarlo."

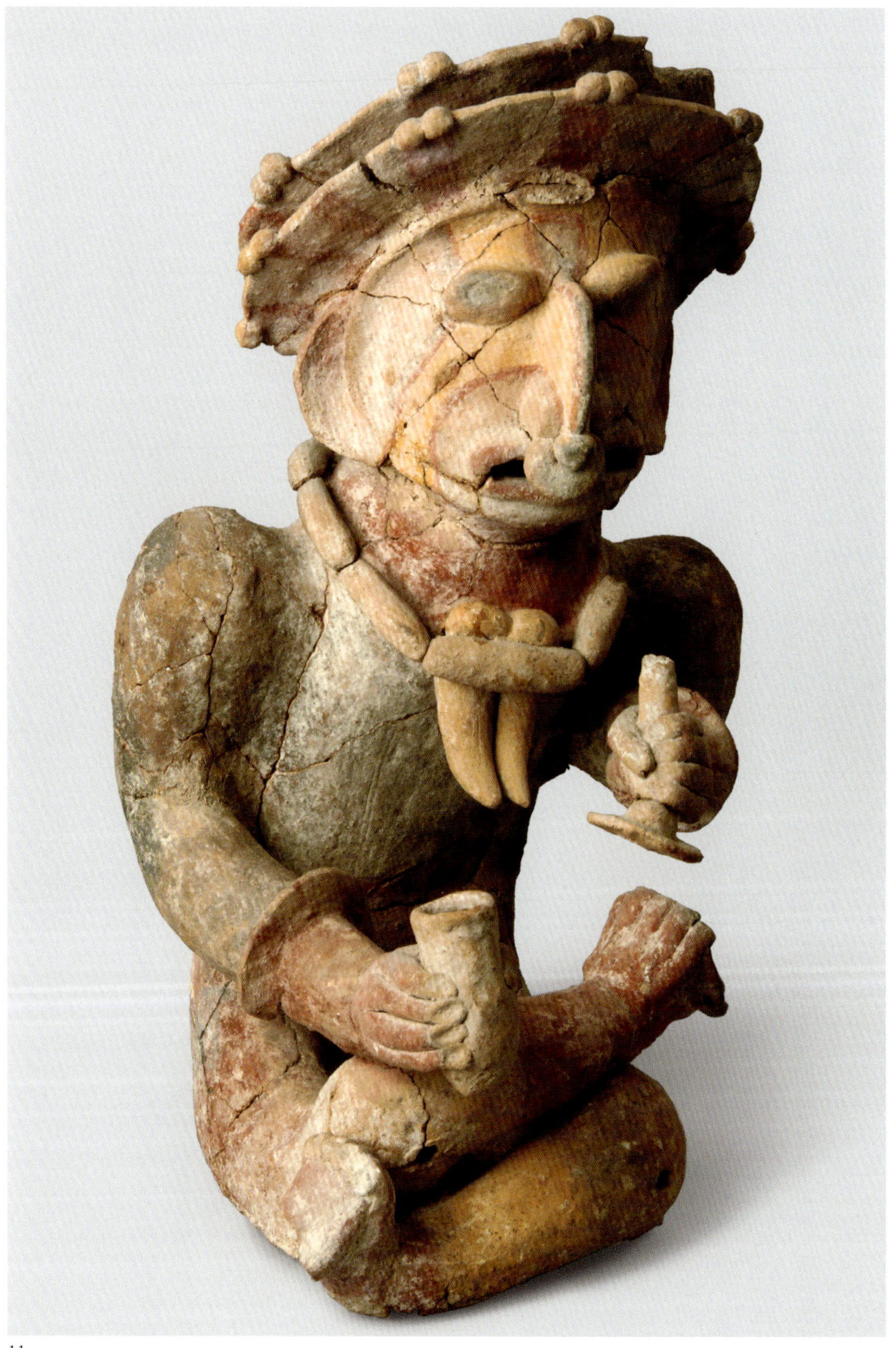

11

[2] Maya 1998, p. 565, no. 186.
[3] *Tesori* 2004, pp. 50, 272 no. 7-11.
[4] *Colombien* 1975, no. 192-198.
[5] *Perù* 2003.
[6] Mason 1961, p. 78.
[7] Lapiner 1976, p. 49, fig. 70; p. 61, fig. 10.
[8] Franch 1958, p. 186.
[9] The chronology of the civilisations of ancient Ecuador is still far from what might be referred to as definitively reliable precision. Every chronological table varies depending on the source used and represents therefore an approximation only. (*Tesori* 1982 = [T]; Cummins & Burgos 1996 = [C&B])

Civilisation	Age	Source
Valdivia	3200–1800 BC	(T)
Machalilla	2000–1000 BC	(T)
Chorrera	1800–300 BC	(T)
Guangala	500 BC–500 AD	(T)
Bahia	500 BC–650 AD	(C&B)
Jama-Coaque I (Regional Development Period)	300/200 BC–700 AD	(C&B)
Jama-Coaque II (Integration Period)	800 AD–1532 AD	(C&B)
The Tolita	600 BC–400 AD	(C&B)
Manteña	500 BC–1532 AD	(C&B)
Empire Inca	1440 AD–1532 AD	

[10] *Tesori* 1982, pp. 75, 104, 105, 107, 113, 126.
[11] Cummins & Burgos 1996.
[12] Collon 1997.
[13] This applies also to equivalent shapes from different, mainly prehistoric, eras that have been recovered in other parts of the world.
[14] Some of the handles of flat *sellos* plans show features of a zoomorphic head (Cummins & Burgos 1996, p. 84, fig. 4a), others feature minute geometric incisions (see file P 52). The specimens under review indicate wear and tear.
[15] See file P 49.
[16] Enciso 1947: XIII cites a specimen originating from Tlatilco (Mesoamerica) 23 cm in height.
[17] *Colombien* 1975: cat. no. 192
[18] *Tesori* 2004, pp. 272, 273; no. 7-11
[19] The term *pintadera* it currently used in Spanish as an alternative or synonym of the word *sello*. Various authors use the two terms together, that is *sellos o pintaderas* (Estrada 1959), or Pre-Columbian *sellos e pintaderas* (Zanetti 1995, p. 114)
[20] *Tesori* 1982, p. 26.
[21] De Landa 1864.
[22] Parducci 1967, p. 143.
[23] Cummins & Burgos 1996, p. 26.
[24] Bodenhorst 1984, p. 27.
[25] D'Harcourt 1962, p. 68.
[26] Cummins & Burgos 1996, p. 31.
[27] Ortegon 1999.
[28] Klein & Cevallos 2007, plate 97, p. 115.
[29] Klein & Cevallos 2007, p. 354.
[30] See C 13, P 38, P 40, P 41, P 43, P 47.
[31] Gonzales 1993, p. 130.
[32] Ricchieri 2002, pp. 78, 79.
[33] Venturoli 2006, p. 26.
[34] Venturoli 2006, p. 27.
[35] Estrada 1959, p. 15.
[36] Field 1967, p. 22.
[37] Gonzales 1993, p. 82.
[38] Gonzales 1993, p. 43.
[39] Zanetti 1995, p. 114.
[40] Cummins & Burgos 1996, p. 34.
[41] Field 1967, p. 22.
[42] Mason 1961, p. 78.
[43] D'Harcourt 1947, p. 67.
[44] Restrepo 1992, p. 27.
[45] On the Ecuadorian coast
[46] Bodenhorst 1984, p. 31.
[47] See C 4, C 5, C 6, C 7, C 8, C 17.
[48] Di Capua 1984, pp. 82–83. The author does not show a reproduction of the figurine. Since the related inventory number refers to the collections of the "Museum of the Central Bank of Ecuador" at Quito, we have asked the Bank to provide us with one. Unfortunately we did not receive an answer to our request.
[49] Cummins & Burgos 1996, p. 65.
[50] Cummins & Burgos 1996, p. 246, figs. 22 a, b.
[51] Estrella E. 1993, cover.
[52] Salomone 1975, p. 114.
[53] Fuhrmann 1922, p. 50.
[54] Laurencich 1983, p. 70.
[55] Guayaquil, Casa de la Cultura Simón Bolívar.
[56] Salomone 1975, p. 117.
[57] Sotheby's 1992, fig. 258.
[58] Sotheby's 1994, fig. 40.
[59] Sotheby's 1989, fig. 50.
[60] *Trésors* 1974, p. 94.
[61] Private collection.
[62] Venturoli 2006, p. 80.

Part II

Iconography of the Ecuadorian *Sellos*

It would seem essential at this point to define a methodological approach dealing with the symbolic system used for the *sellos* by the ancient civilisations of Ecuador – e.g. the compilation of a database of symbols and morphology of the patterns. The main methodological studies concerning the *sellos* of the Meso-American cultures are those of Enciso[63] and particularly those of Franch[64] and of Field[65] as well as the recently published work of Ladron.[66]

Wherever possible it would seem important to establish a classification of the morphemic groups present in the *sellos* and to attempt to produce an interpretation. This presents obvious inherent difficulties, for the objects, while taking their cue from reality, tend towards abstraction and only seldom show any tendency towards purely decorative functions. "On the other hand artisanal 'decorative' patterns are not popular creations, as one might tend to believe, rather they constitute perfectly established and ceremonially repeated patterns, traditional symbols revealing thought and cosmogonical concepts."[67] Indeed, careful observation of their composition suggests an order that is the expression of abstract symbolic references (in the etymological sense of the term) that every design expresses within itself. They represent stylisations of concepts and images from the real world, which are, at times, hardly recognisable as anthropo-zoomorphic figures, or something unknown. Sometimes a certain ambiguity arises from the tension between shapes that are purely abstract and patterns which in reality appear as such because they are stylised representations so closely associated and composed as to make a reading of the patterns on the *sellos* quite difficult.

Equally difficult would be the capacity to grasp the intended synthesis with which they were conceived. So-called primitive civilizations never adopted the concept of 'art for art's sake' as part of their culture. Every artistic expression is tightly bound to the representation of symbolically expressed concepts. "The artist of those times did not mean to provide a naturalistic representation. Pre-Hispanic art was aimed at the representation of a number of

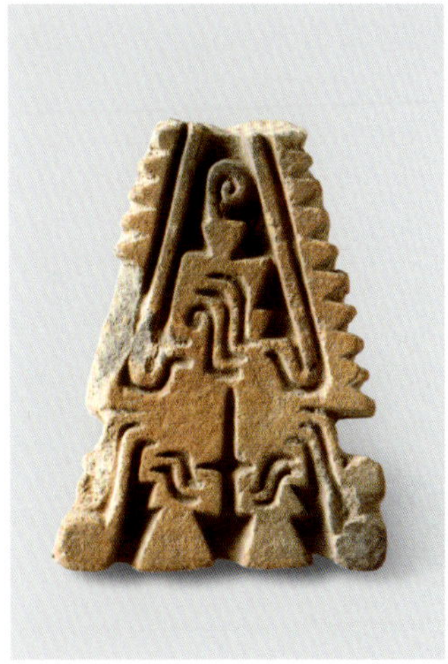

P 18

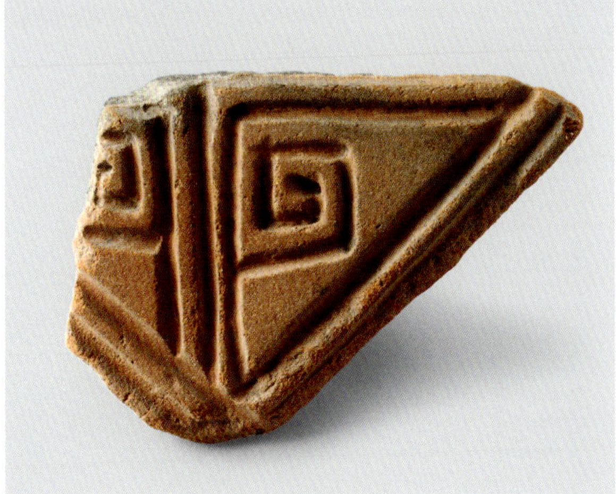

P 27

motifs possessing sacred meanings. They are not always immediately readable and not all are accessible."[68] These considerations must lead us to compile some of the recurring styles or themes which we have encountered in order to proffer a meaning or an identity which might have been previously overlooked.

While compiling these recurring stylistic features we should emphasise that they only represent morphemes of a language – individual words whose meaning mainly escapes us. In order to engage in a meaningful discourse we would need to connect these words to each other in accordance with a syntax whose rules, however, are unknown to us. Only then would they articulate a complete and comprehensible discourse. It is no accident that they come together in every single *sello*, which is thus a composition, a compilation of more than one image.

The specific meaning of the art of Ecuadorian *sellos* remains a mystery, in the sense that there is no image that might be unequivocally identified in terms intended by its creator. Many scholars have attempted to identify the key which might unlock the interpretation of the cultural symbolism typical of beliefs, mythology, and ideology of Pre-Columbian America. "Small statuettes stare at the observer with ferocious eyes, intimidate him with their frowning and stern eyebrows; piercing fangs protrude from enormous snouts and sharp claws extend challengingly. As we inhale

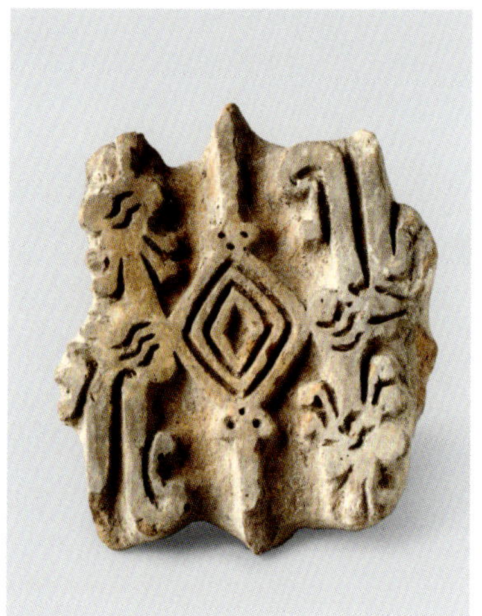

P 26

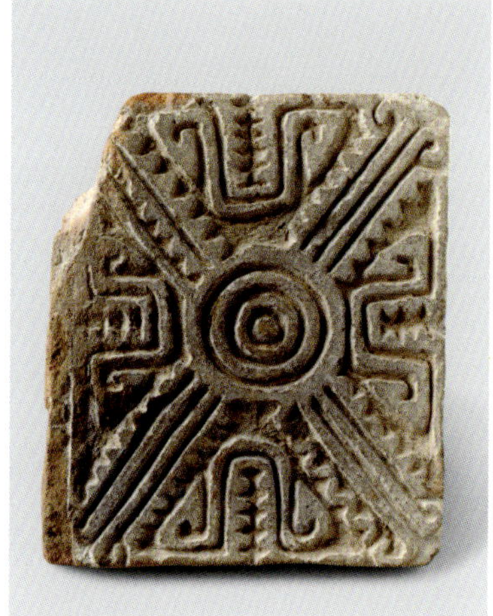

P 53

the breath of these clay monsters we experience deep respect for the unknown."[69]

As one attempts a definition of their meaning one might try to establish links between the various patterns that have been created, and this may be achieved through a comparative study that begins with some of the main elementary geometric patterns present in *sellos*. They deserve further and detailed interpretative analysis on the basis of a different syntax with which they re-appear in the various *sellos*.

Triangular shapes whose background indicates an upward or downward direction might thus express a synthesis of reciprocal vertical tensions consistent with a metaphysical concept of reality (**figs. P 18, P 27**).

The lozenge is another recurrent elementary geometric pattern evident in several *sellos*. Its characteristic pointed arrow-like configuration traditionally represents a symbol directed to the four spatial coordinates, and this may find expression in numerous declinations (**fig. P 26**).

One observes various typologies of squares. According to tradition the square symbolically represents the four corners of the earth and the created world. "For Pre-Columbian civilizations, the world was a square plane surrounded by the sea; a sort of island, which fused with the celestial dome at the line of the horizon."[70] (**fig. P 53**)

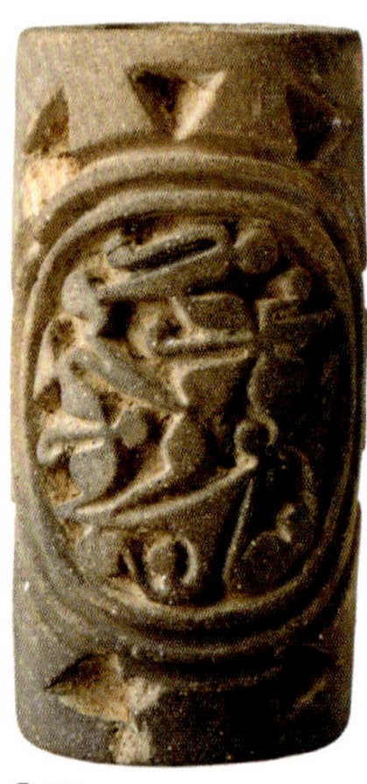

C 19

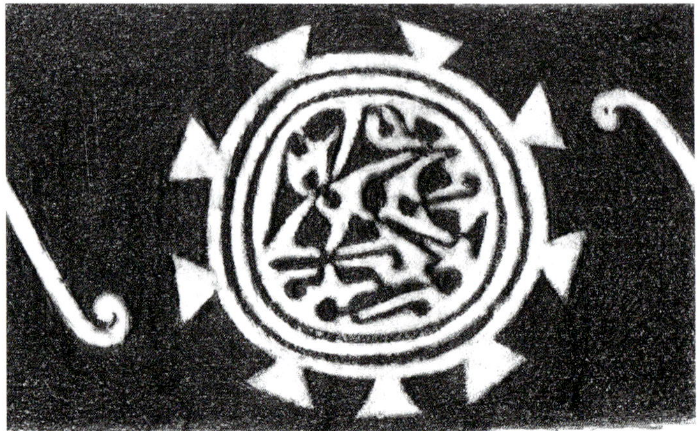

In every culture the circular pattern expresses a heavenly symbol, with the sun as its emblem[71]; it is the cosmic wheel always spinning and evolving, thus illustrating life's transcendental meaning. Once more this is a synthesis of the theme of a radiating centre exuding vital energy. The meaning of a cylindrical *sello* is unambiguous: it shows a radiating circle in the shape of a toothed wheel – the symbol of eternal evolution – which envelops a world consisting of a set of enigmatic figures (**fig. C 19**). We delude ourselves that the wheel within which the inexorable whorl of the shapes occurs is actually stationary.

In several *sellos* we find a set of varied lineal elements, meanderings, convolutions that generally combine and intersect in a most intricate and tangled fashion. They represent developments of elements that become truly free shapes placed in continuity to form enigmatic sets.

From a merely geometric point of view, the spiral is represented by a line that expands and develops centrifugally as it emerges from the centre. In this way, it takes on the character of the traditional symbol of ongoing genesis that arises from a beginning or, on the contrary, coils centripetally toward its end.

The S-shaped pattern, one of the most recurrent and important images, consists of a bar that curls in opposite directions at both ends. While a spiral represents expansion and development, the feature that connects symmetrically opposed curls, on the other hand, seems to imply a union of opposites; it thus takes on the traditional meaning of conciliation and unity. "Within these concepts another fundamental element of 'life' in the Andes finds its expression: it is the couple, the number two, in other words the union of the masculine and feminine, and all other complementary opposites that give origin to life and yield stability, and which are the foundation on which of Andean society was built."[72] This whole world is infused with the concept of complementary opposites serving as a witness to order and stability.[73]

The stylisation of the subject may be carried to the point where it becomes extremely abstract; yet the interpretative results are no longer ambiguous and may be subject to debate. It could well be taken as the representation of the plumed serpent (**fig. C 21**).

Segmented linear patterns make use of zigzag lines. The angles may be right or acute; the lines may be hooked or may end in distortion or wrap into a spiral. Sometimes a segment bends itself into a hook while the opposite side ends in a sort of plume (**fig. C 20**). This might suggest an abstract, albeit emblematic,

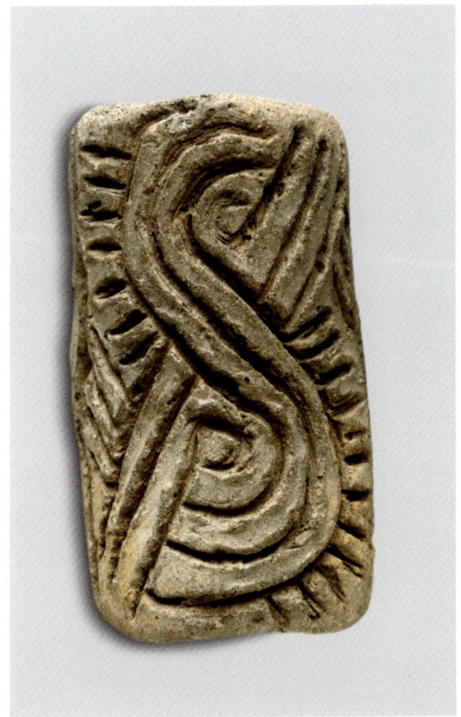

C 21

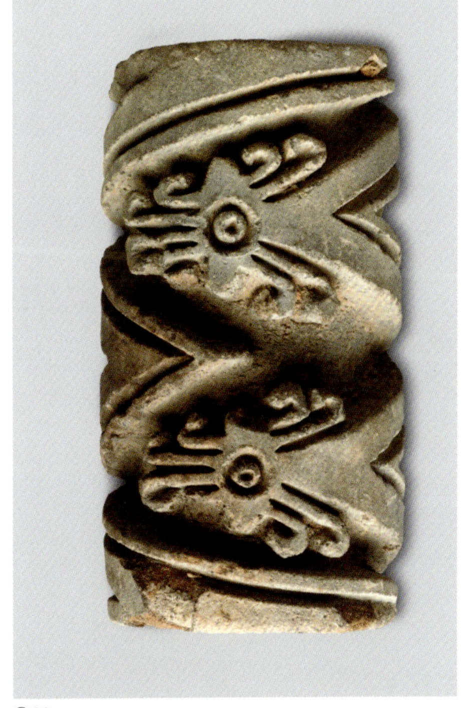

C 20

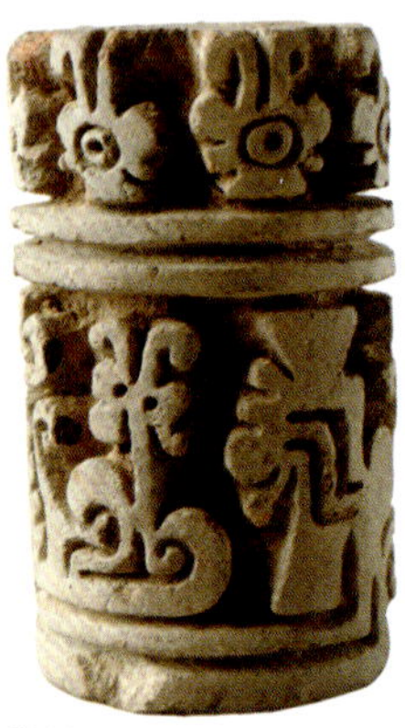

C 22

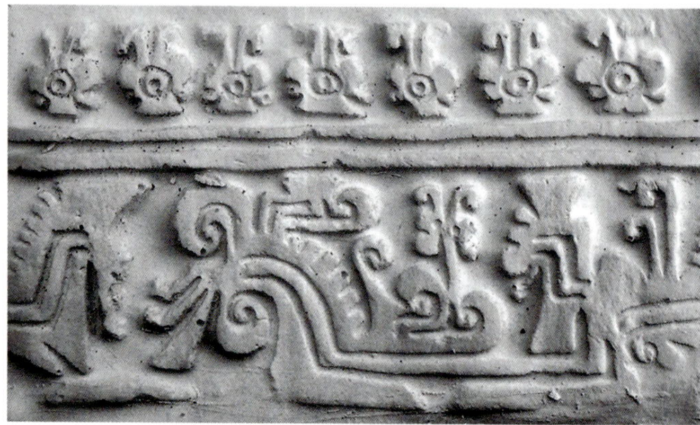

styling of the mythical image of the plumed serpent, which is a typical totemic image in Pre-Columbian culture[74] – the union of what slithers on the earth and what flies in the sky, hence the union of opposites (**fig. C 22**).[75]

The zoomorphic patterns that are present in *sellos* clearly indicate the fondness of ancient people for cults that involve various animal species. They are often adopted as totemic figures. One may wonder at the remarkable supernatural qualities they exhibit – possessing powers and performing feats far superior to those of humans. The symbolic function of transcendent totemic energies was thus translated into the shapes of animals. However: *"...sería temerario definirlos categóricamente como tal o cual animal, solamente se puede decir que son representaciones zoomorfas."*[76] For the animals carved in *sellos* are often highly stylised; this renders their specific identification difficult, even though it is not uncommon to detect characteristic elements of certain species.

In particular we may observe zoomorphic figures closely reflecting various species of the marine world; or we may view birds and animals in mirrored images (**see cat. P 51**). Other figures appear to be enigmatic, mirrored with regard to the *sello*'s axis, either symmetrically or facing opposite ends, with huge encircled eyes, a wrinkled nose and huge snouts that protrude from bodies whose erect tails curls upward.[77] These are complex fantasized interpretations in which the image may be read as the merging of two zoomorphic entities; alternatively they may be read as one single mask (**see cat. P 40, P 41, P 43, P 51**).

Anthropomorphic Iconography in Ecuadorian *Sellos*

A preliminary remark may be appropriate at this point. It is entirely possible that each piece may have a different story to tell. Nothing is known of the maker's skills. Was he or she recognized as a professional, or was the creator perhaps simply a more or less gifted artisan eking out a life producing objects on request or even for a specific market, or possibly he was simply a self-made craftsman with limited skills, a priest or shaman who undertook engraving as a sideline?

Anthropomorphic iconography warrants an in-depth analysis as an illustration of the extreme variety of symbolic representations and of the numerous themes we encounter in *sellos*.

In its most elementary form, in cylindrical *sellos* the human figure is drawn frontally, naked, without sexual attributes (hence as 'human') by means of a plain incision (**fig. C 1**). The head is a circle within which the eyes are sometimes marked as dots; the body is a vertical line bifurcating into two legs, or it is depicted by two lines bending outward to signify feet; the shoulders are horizontal lines bending downward at an angle of 90° to represent arms. Human figures crowd a confined space between slanted patterns featuring hooks and toothing. These patterns are difficult

C 1
Impression
as positive
(above right)
and impression
as negative
(below right)

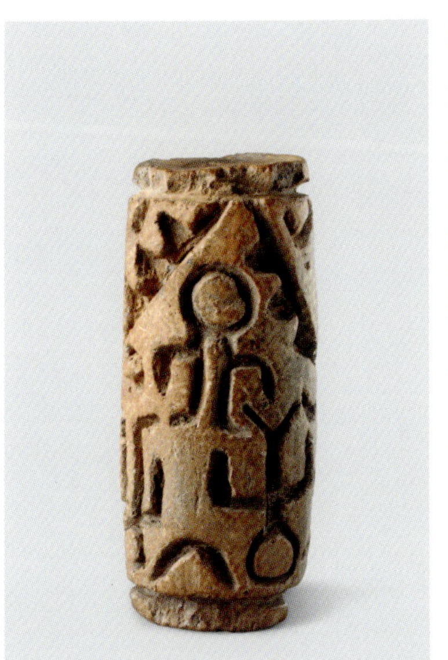

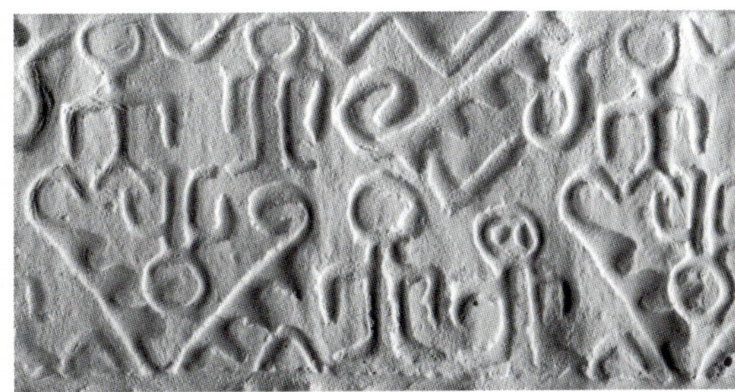

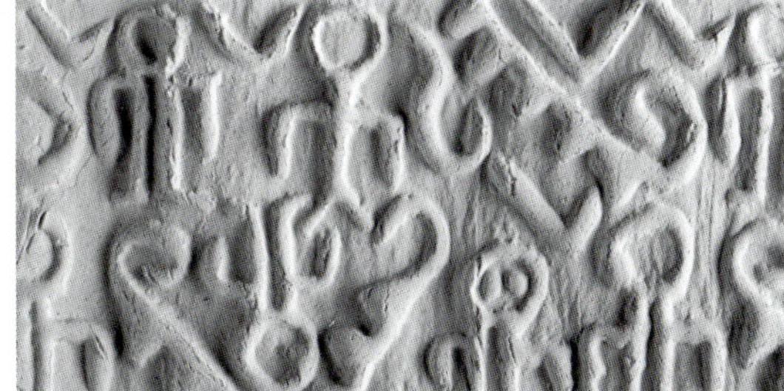

C 1

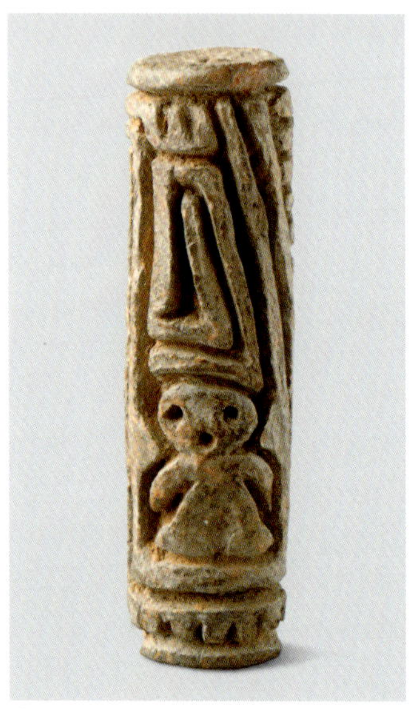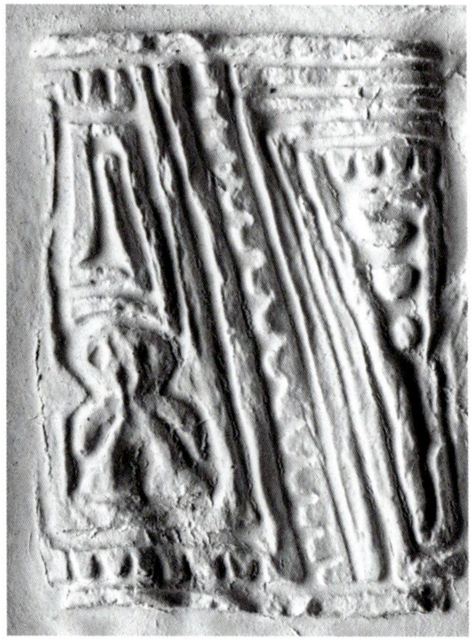

C 2

to interpret. One might read them as representing a bird's-eye view of people stretched out, thereby implying that the figures as drawn in the opposite direction.[78] *Sellos* with human figures, however, usually show mono-directional reading that would indicate the pre-ordained directionality of the *sello*.

A greater anatomical precision is obtained when the mouth is shown as an additional point within the face, while the limbs are no longer schematic (**fig. C 2**). Here the head is prominent in comparison to the body. Above all, the symbolic-religious character of the human figure is strengthened by its association with shapes and symbols such as the tall pointed helmet, its spiralled pattern terminating in a trident. One might perceive the human figure somehow to be an emanation of the spiralled helmet.

The representation of twinned figures is particularly fraught with meaning that may relate to the origin of a culture: "... being two, they originated from within the same single egg, thus symbolizing the dual manifestation of the same principle ..."[79] The twinned figures symbolize the dialectic play of the cosmos, which transforms itself into unifying couples: "... both centrifugal and centripetal forces continuously fulfil their aim of stability and order through the mediation of the binary and the complementarity of the opposites which they exemplify."[80] The morphology is once more one of frontal figures holding hands (if placed inside a double tier, the images may be placed symmetrically along a horizontal axis, indicating the double directionality of the *sello*) (**fig. C 4**). More attention is given to the characterisation of chest and limbs; also the head may lose its circular shape (**fig. C 3**). Distinctive ambiguous graphemes or zoomorphic images (monkeys)[81] (**fig. C 16**) may be associated with them; they are found together with a slanted dotted sequence that divides the surface into equal and distinct banded boxes with toothed and spiralled patterns. We even have examples of figures (not holding hands) who wear a loincloth[82]; they show a clear schematic representation of fingers and toes as well as a navel.

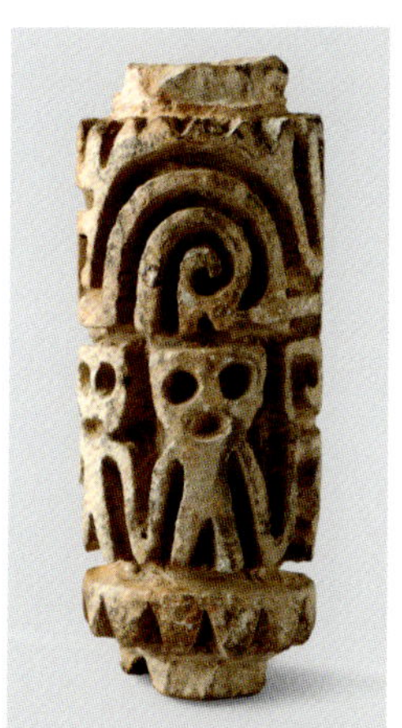

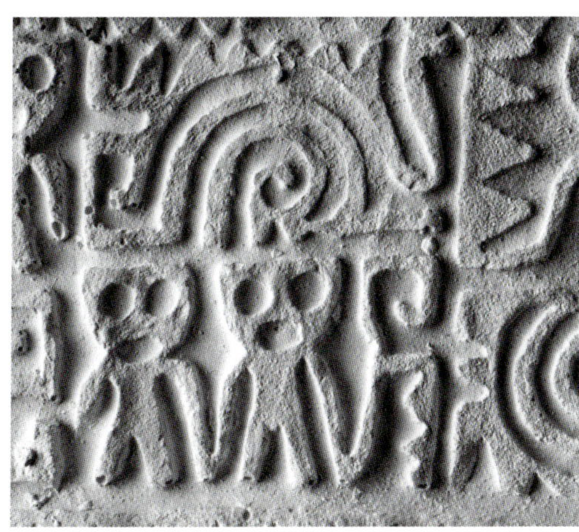

C 3

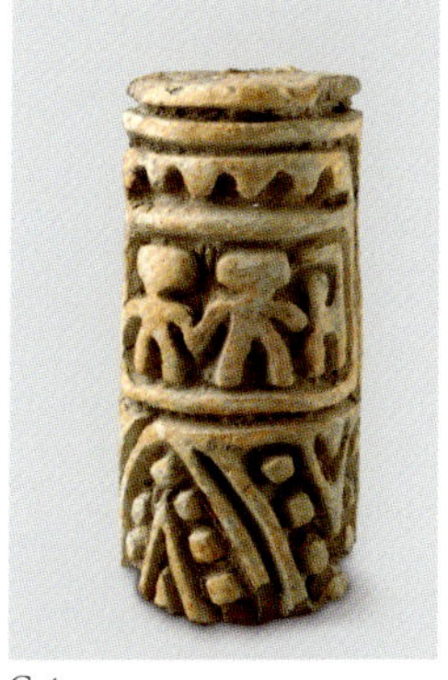

C 4

C 16

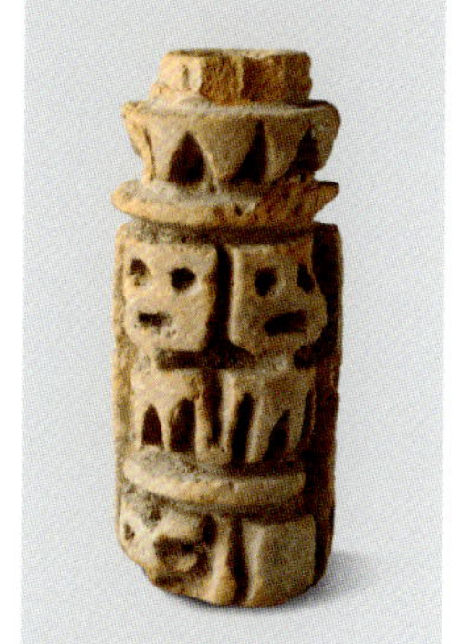

C 17

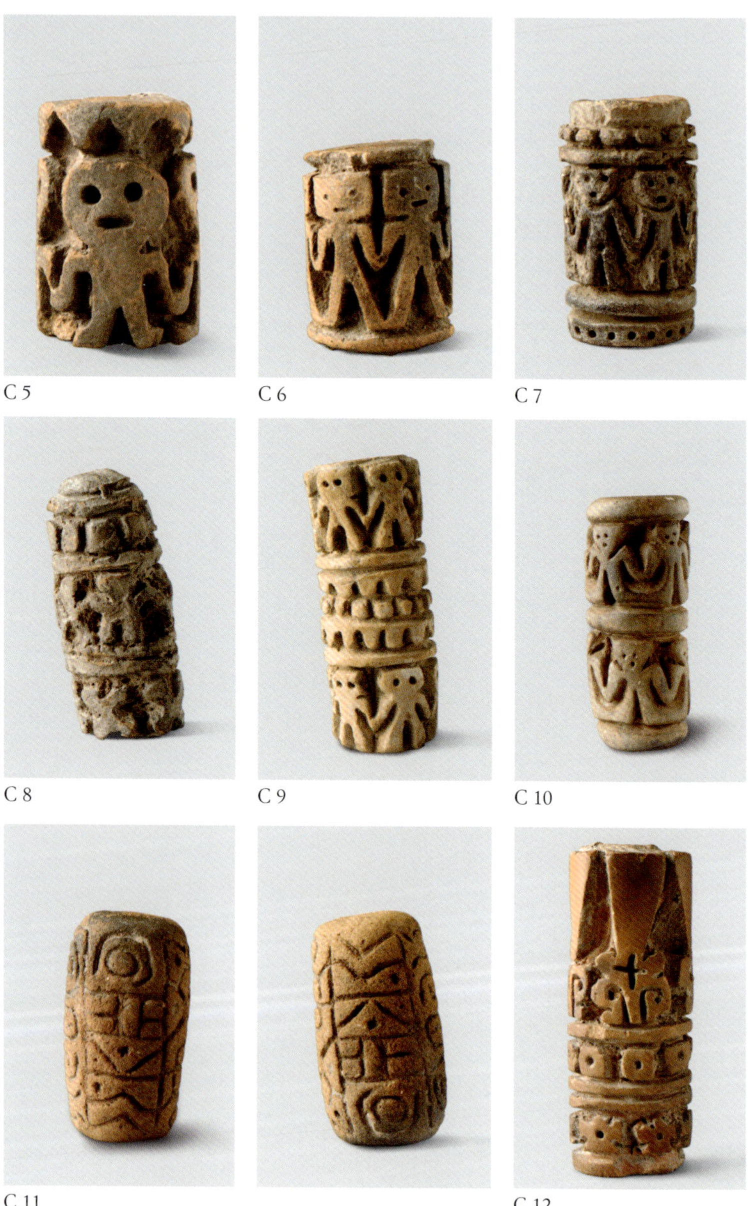

C 5

C 6

C 7

C 8

C 9

C 10

C 11

C 12

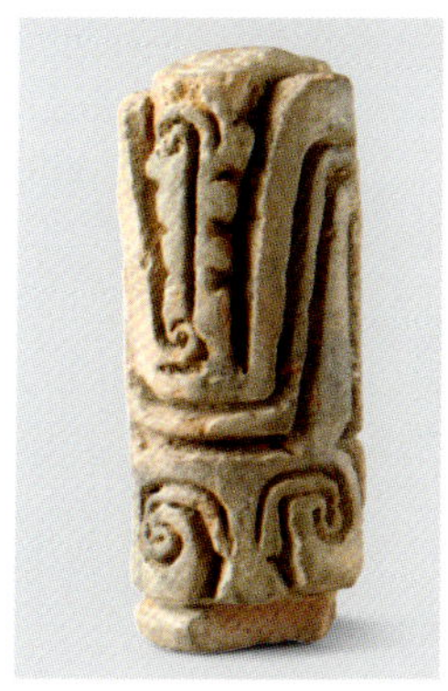
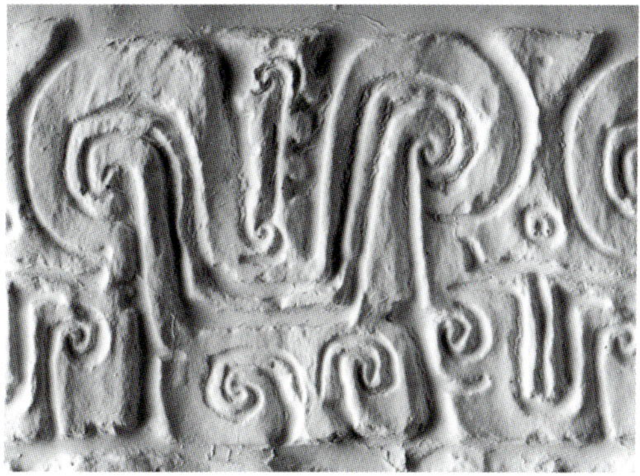

C 13

In cylindrical *sellos* the number of frontal figures may range from two to groups of three,[83] or of four[84]; however, they are clearly meant to represent a continuous sequence that somehow repeats itself[85] (**figs. C 5–C 10**).

One can detect numerous variations on the same theme: the arms droop, less frequently rarely they point upward[86] (**fig. C 8**); legs may be straight and vertical, or spread apart; they may touch the limbs of the adjacent figures (**figs. C 6, C 10**) or not (**figs. C 5, C 9**). Figures may be placed in one or more tiers[87] (**figs. C 9–C 10**); they may be mirrored across a horizontal plane.[88] They may seem to represent a ritual or ceremony, in which men and women – mostly naked or simply wearing a loincloth – alternate. They may express an art form which is ritual, or represent collective manifestations of a live and harmonious universe. At times mysterious stylized images with step-like excretions or engraved double S patterns may alternate with a row of anthropomorphic figures holding hands.[89] Often they are further associated with simple or toothed bands; additionally we may find a series of dots, spiral patterns or a free-flowing row of four-cornered images which may sometimes look like four-petalled flowers viewed frontally.

Some of the cylindrical *sellos* portray the human face only – frontally or sideways – rather than the entire figure; unambiguous and characteristic stylizations – segmented or curvilinear traits – are represented in the image (**fig. C 11**).

We should, however, exercise utmost interpretative caution in all instances. As an example, one might be confronted with a

V-shaped pattern that curls out at the ends: one might then read into it orbs and a long nose suggestive of a mask. But the same pattern in other *sellos* might have a totally different, if unknown, meaning. Thus, in some cylindrical *sellos* this pattern is strongly emphasized (**figs. C 12–C 13**) and associated with ring-shaped bands interspersed with sequences of dotted circles and star-like patterns. Here the pattern may represent a stylized mask characterized by a high curled head-gear somewhat reminiscent of animal horns.

In flat *sellos* featuring anthropomorphic figures their surface and the figures coincide. We may begin with a representation of the basic human figure (**fig. P 1**), where a vertical staff represents the body from which sprout arms and legs. The head is a knob set on top of the staff; stylized radiating plumage creates a sort of halo. A similar motif is placed atop a highly stylized figure with arms raised in a position denoting prayer (**fig. P 2**).

In other flat *sellos* the human figure, while still depicted frontally, appears in greater detail, even hinting at fingers and toes, or with holes in the auricular lobes; curved bands protrude all around the profile (laterally as well at the top and bottom) as if to signify an aura emanating from the body (**fig. P 4**). An arm with an asymmetric articulation may be an attempt to portray the figure in motion (**fig. P 5**) while retaining the static element of the plumed helmet.

The human figure often plays an intermediary role between the forces of nature: by using masks or shamanic disguises man

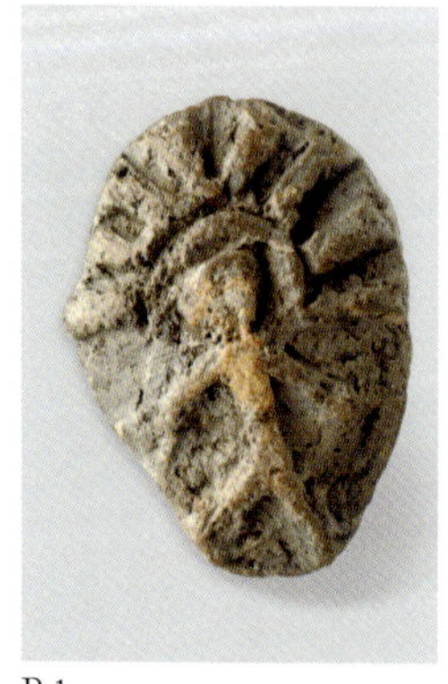

P 1

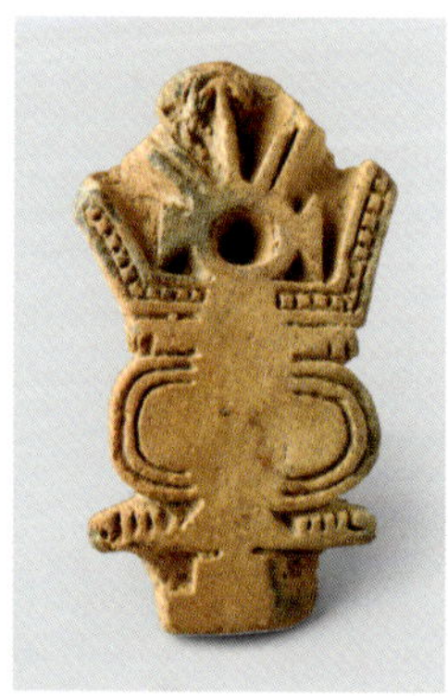

P 2

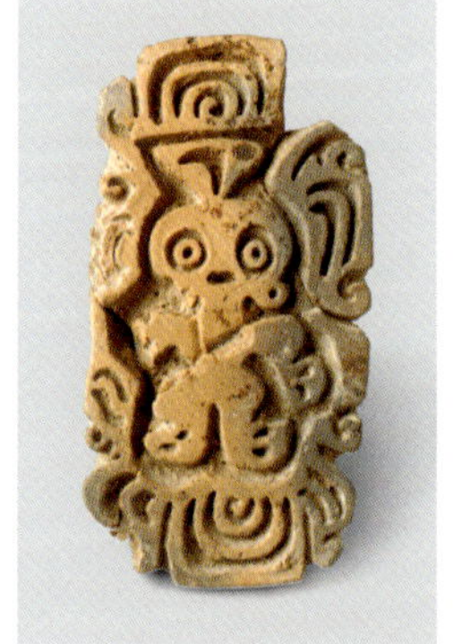

P 4

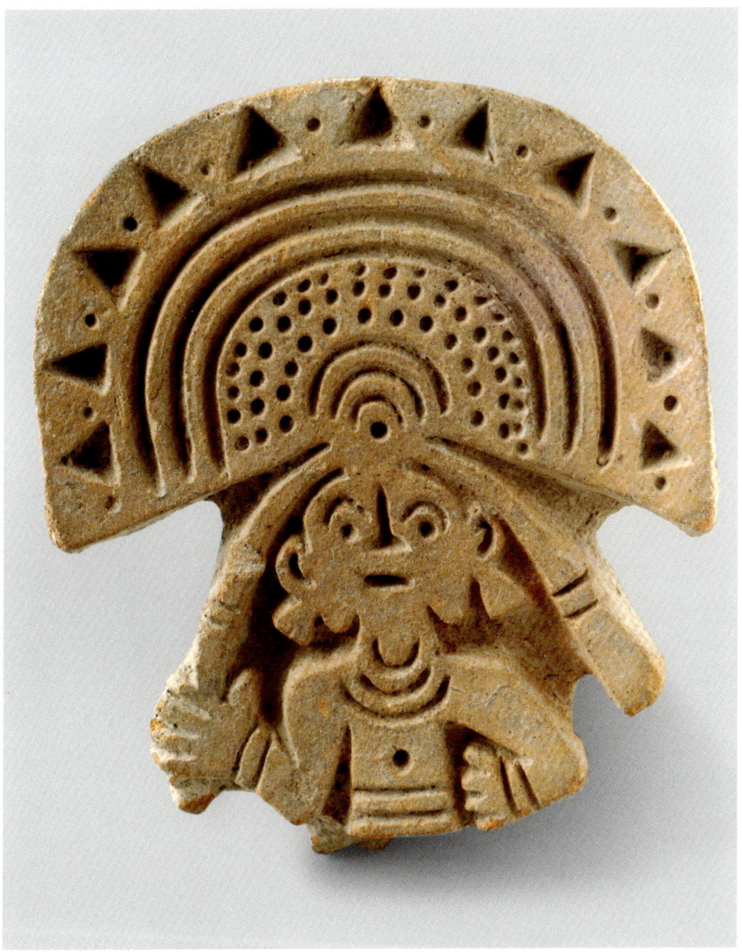

P 5

assumes animal attributes. Given the number of recoveries of such objects we may see them as widely used fetishes playing an important role in the transmission of symbolically codified ideas. The symbolic-religious representation of the human figure gains in strength when placed in association with figures and symbols, even though the latter may be difficult to interpret.

Most native peoples used (and still use) animal disguises in their initiation ceremonies and rituals. In *sellos* such figures are portrayed frontally or with a frontal chest; the head and legs however are often shown in profile[90] and these guises may even include an ornamental tail (**figs. P 6–P 9, P 11–P 13, P 48**).

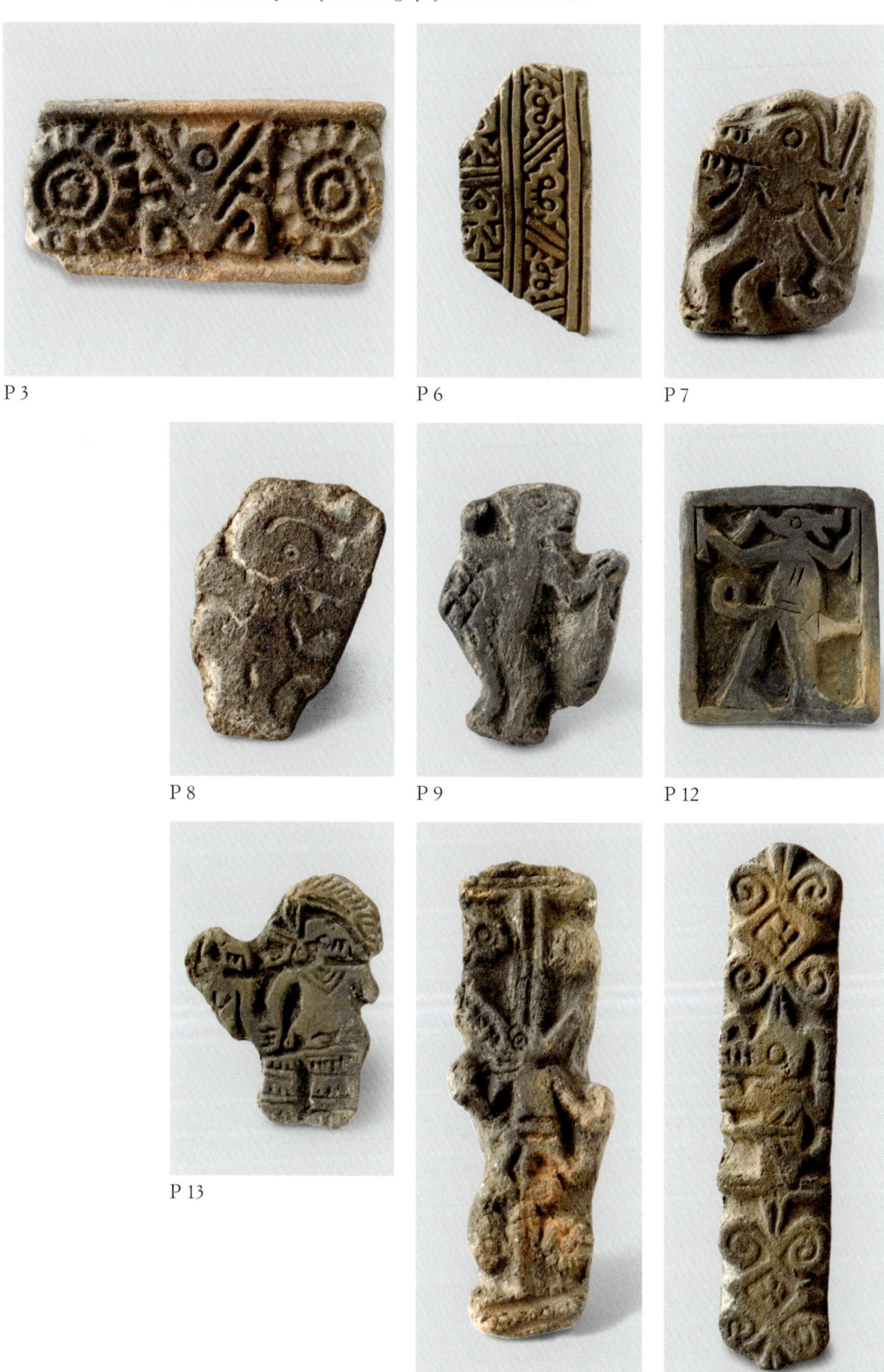

P 3

P 6

P 7

P 8

P 9

P 12

P 13

P 11

P 48

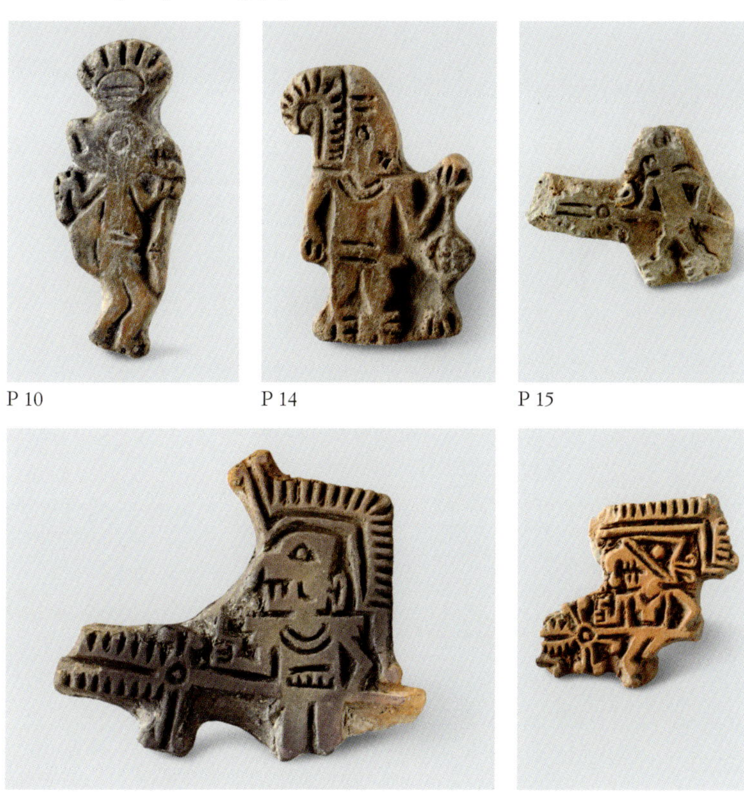

P 10   P 14   P 15

P 16   P 17

When they are shown in full profile these figures in disguised form may hold a sort of harpoon in their left hand[91] (**figs. P 10, P 14**) or they may grasp with the two hands a trophy-tipped staff[92]; the images may reveal in their movements the craftsman's capacity for careful naturalistic observation of physical dynamics.

By contrast another series of *sellos* pursues the enhanced stylization of the human figure by highlighting its most characteristic elements (head and limbs), which are typically portrayed in a rather schematic fashion. The stylization chooses geometric form over naturalistic imagery, thus creating an 'abstraction' in the etymological sense of the term – an 'invention' of forms that simply takes the realistic form as a point of departure. The representation becomes increasingly hermetic – to the point of modifying the shapes from which it took its original cue. Some scholars manage to perceive traces of a human figure in *sellos* devoid of naturalistic references and in which the stylization reaches an extreme level of abstraction (**fig. P 18**),[93] where any essential somatic feature may have virtually disappeared (**fig. P 2**). Any direct figurative reference is either wholly or partially dispensed with in the final figurative stylization.

A series of anthropomorphic representations employs the triangular shape to represent the face; the apex points downward and one finds inside characteristics signifying eyes and nose.[94] These representations are so utterly stylized – the arms are bent downward and the legs stand together – that they no longer correspond to a visible reality. The imitative replication

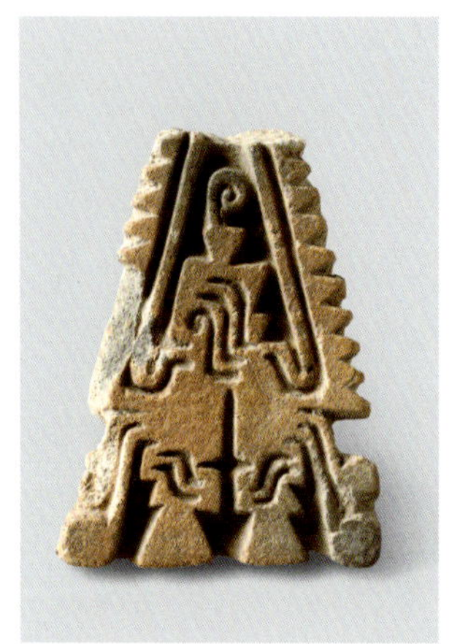

P 18

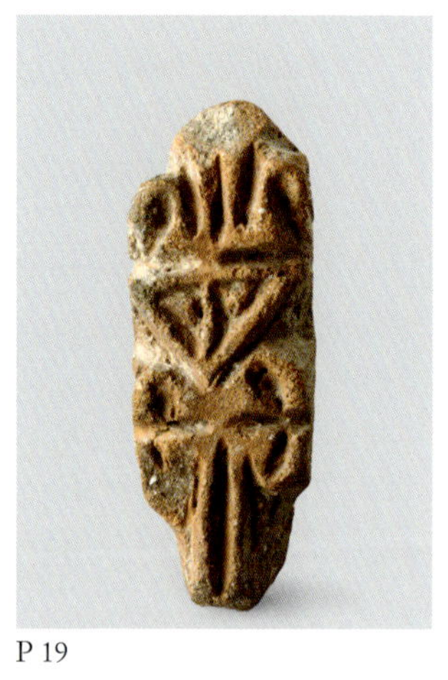

P 19

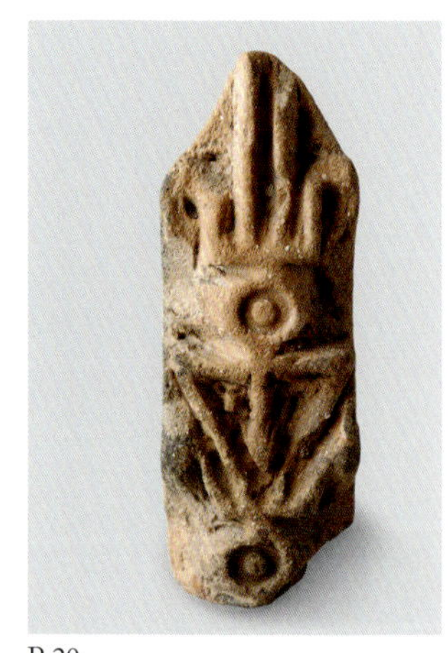

P 20

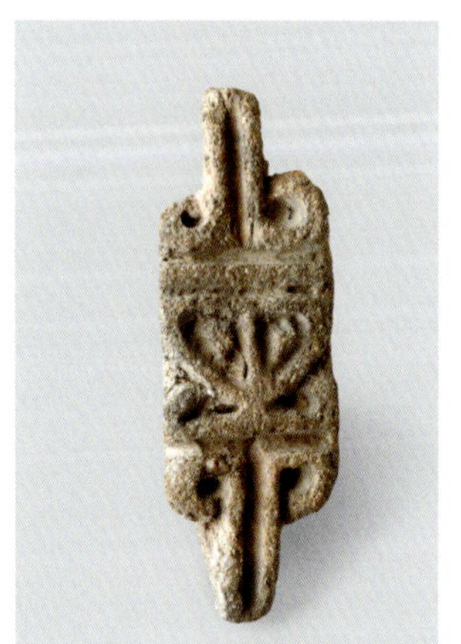

P 21

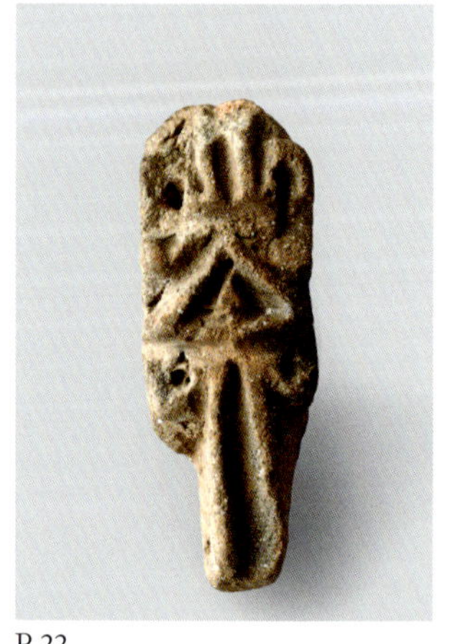

P 22

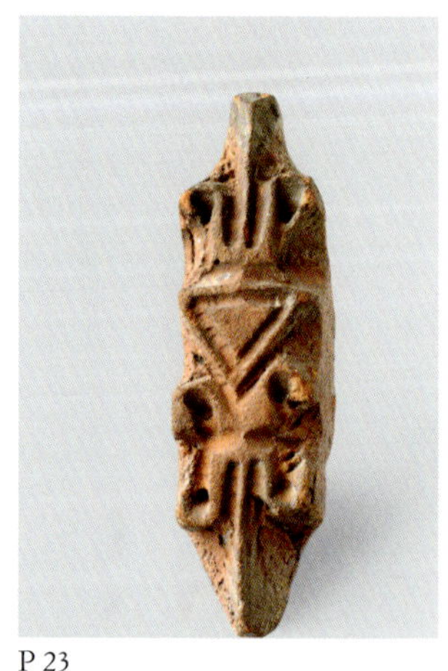

P 23

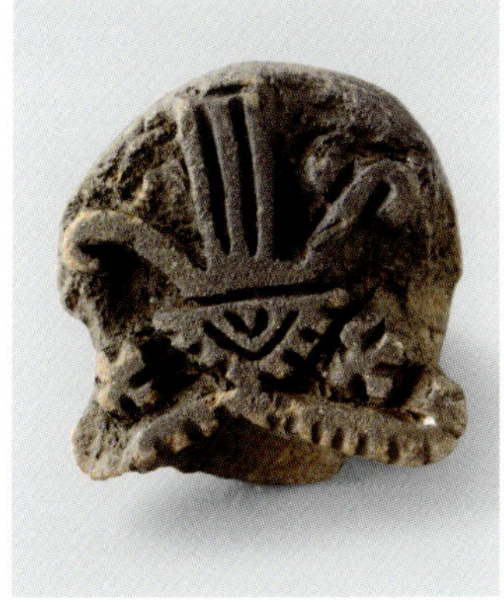

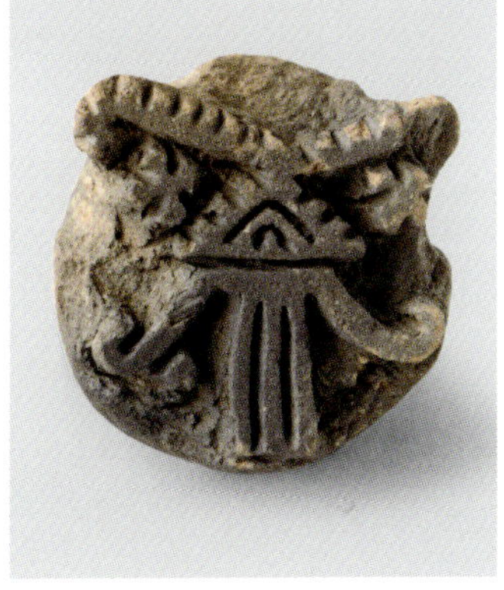

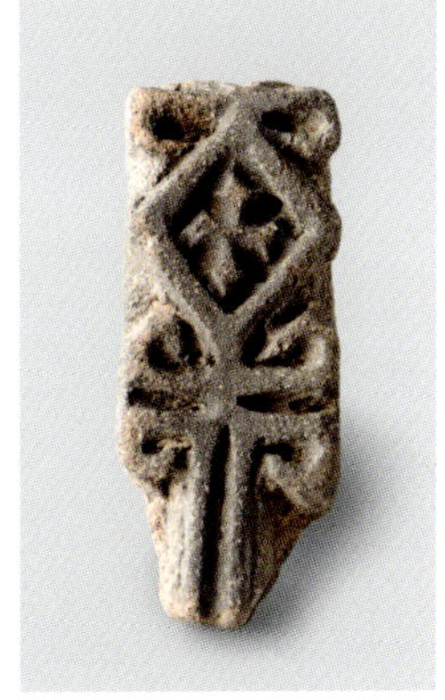

P 24

P 28

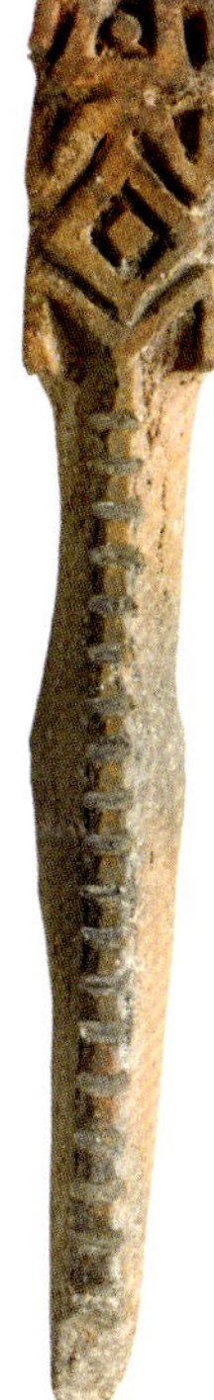

P 25

of the initial model may typically yield further simplifications and modifications or even the deletion of physical traits – as when conventional replication overlooks original and essential elements of the original meaning (**figs. P 22–P 23**). The head is adorned with an imposing plumed headdress with the plumes extending outwards; it takes on a mirrored pattern in respect to the axis of the figure; the arms are bent downward and the legs together (**fig. P 19**).

Given the complete abstraction of the image – now without any direct figurative reference – one would find the interpretation of other *sellos* in which a triangular figure appears to be entirely enigmatic, were it not for the occasional presence – even though in a different form – of the triangle and some stylistic features that typically adorn flat anthropomorphic *sellos* (**fig. P 24**).

Another utterly stylized frontal figure stands at the top of a sequence of dots (**fig. P 25**); its abdomen is a stylized rhombus.[95] This lozenge pattern is a recurrent theme in various anthropomorphic *sellos* – even though it is independently present in other exclusively geometric *sellos*. It is not by accident that the rhombus is placed where the navel of the figure ought to be.[96] Considering its characteristic angular configuration, the rhombus traditionally symbolises vitality pointing out toward the four spatial coordinates. The rhombus (or lozenge) thus becomes the origin of any expanding movement; enclosing, at times, a crossed pattern, thus underscoring the shape's intrinsic geometry[97] (**fig. P 28**).

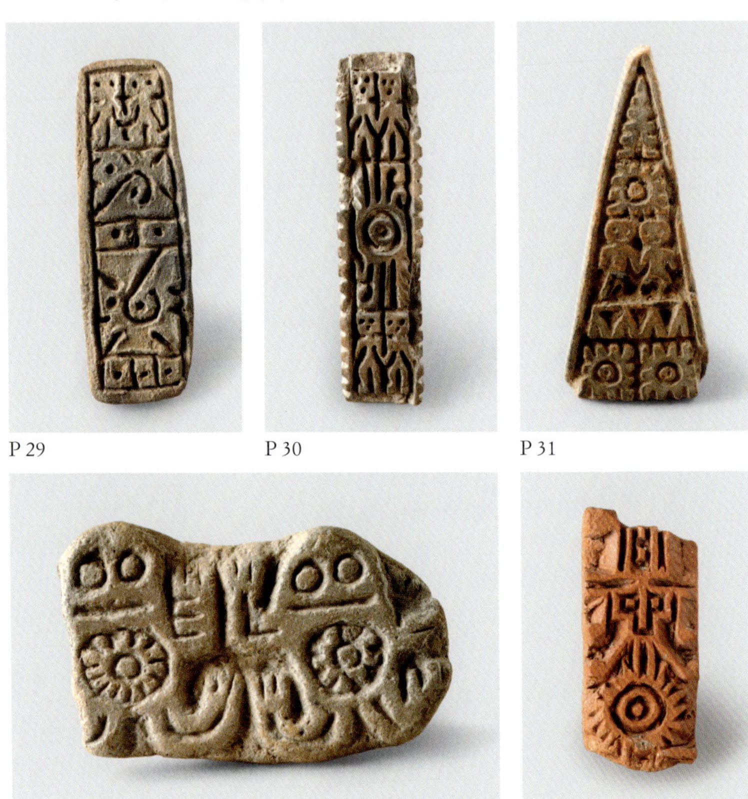

P 29 P 30 P 31

P 32 P 33

We also notice the representation of twinned figures in flat *sellos* – they may be rectangular or triangular in shape thus creating an upward directionality (**fig. P 30**). Particularly meaningful here is the fact that they are usually linked to what are unquestionably solar patterns expressed by circular radiating figures (**fig. P 31**) – even though these figures may feature different patterns; alternatively they may be associated with totemic figures (**fig. P 29**) with or without wings – symbols of cosmic attributes.

Given its evident connection to the origin of life, it is significant that the solar motif is placed to mark the navel of certain figures. Their mouths are represented by a horizontal slash (**fig. P 32**); their posture may appear to signify prayer; they may, on the other hand, simply represent a geometric stylization (**fig.**

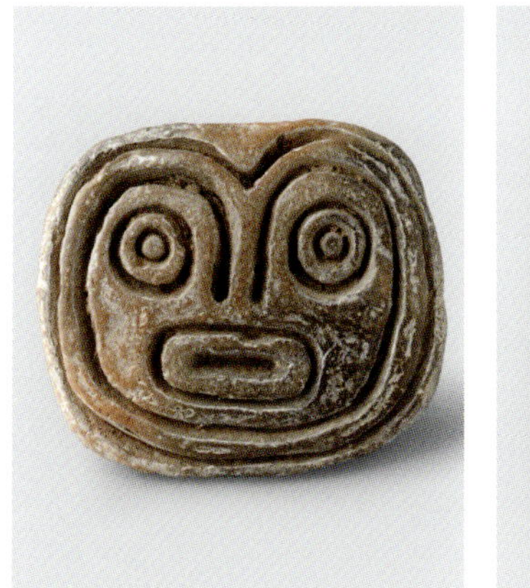

P 34

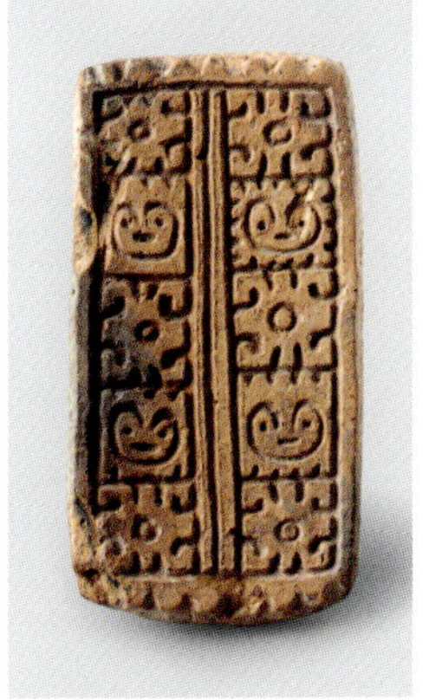

P 35

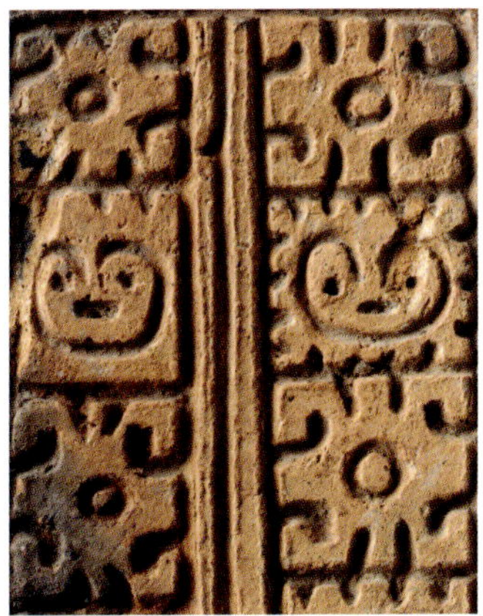

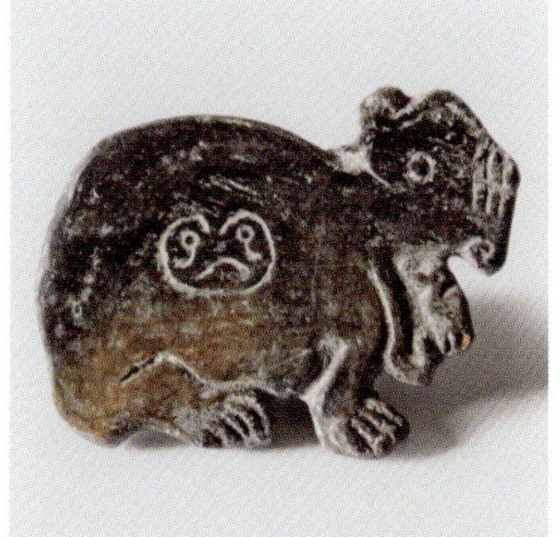

P 37

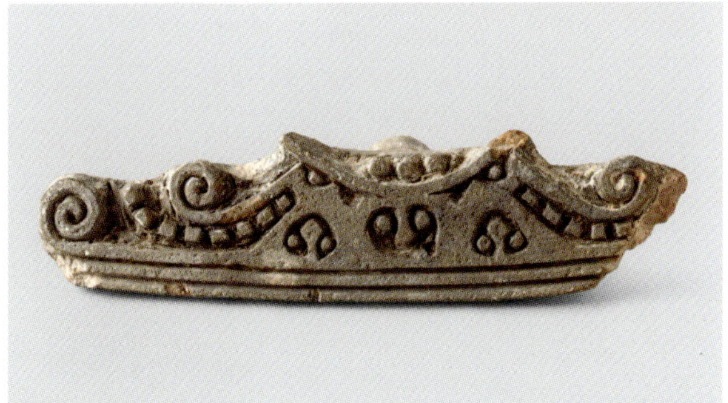

P 36

P 33). The recurrence of concentric shapes that extend sequentially is an indication of their enduring expansion[98]; this is further underlined by the addition of rays emanating in all directions.[99]

Some *sellos* depict emblematic frontal representation of just the human face rather than the whole figure. These are peculiar and characteristic stylizations where the face is enclosed in an oval in which the superciliar arcs, as they encircle circular eyes, extend to the centre to form the line of the nose (**fig. P 34**). The representation sometimes may include linear rays[100] (**fig. P 35**); alternatively it may be enclosed in radiating squares. The motif may be expanded to show part of the chest[101] or inserted as an imprint (**fig. P 37**). Finally, as a filler for empty spaces, a series of faces may appear in alternating directions (**fig. P 36**).

The representation of the face might suggest geometric and highly abstract schematicizations (**figs. P 38–P 39, P 41–P 42**) such as when twin mirrored and squared spirals (rotating to the left and right) converge from opposite polarities along the *sello*'s axis of symmetry thereby essentially concealing the features of the face (**fig. P 38**). Elsewhere, complex fantastical interpretations[102] create an image that, when taken as a whole, might be identified as a face or mask; it might also be taken as a double image, however, it would then necessarily be read as two entities mirrored around a central axis, thereby yielding other (zoomorphic) interpretations. An ambivalent visual effect is obtained where simultaneously complementary images comprise each other and vice versa (**figs. P 40, P 43**).

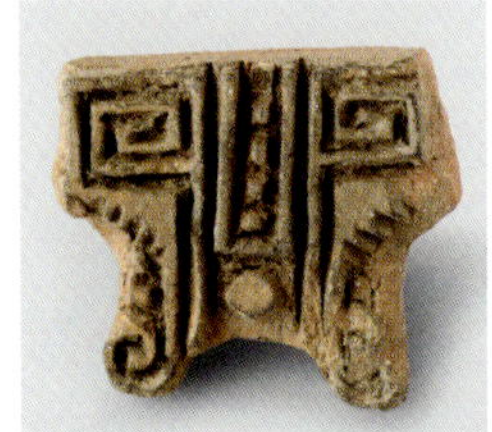

P 38

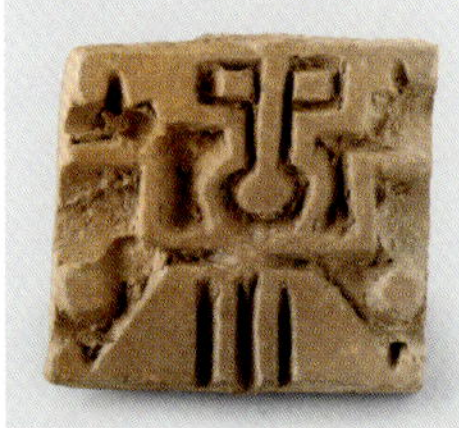

P 39

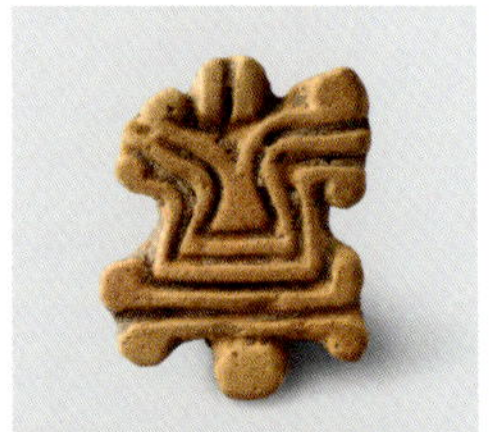

P 42

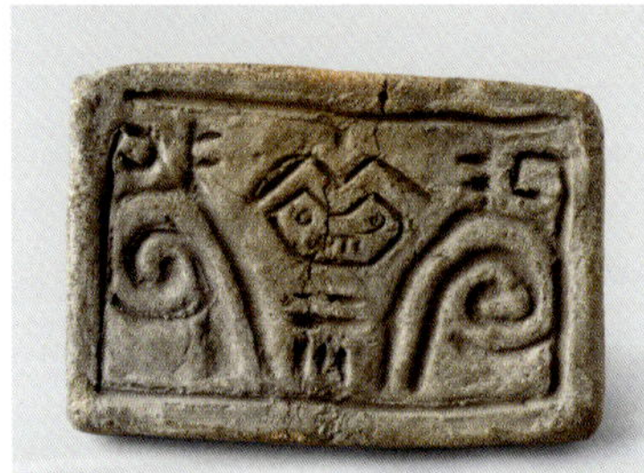

P 41

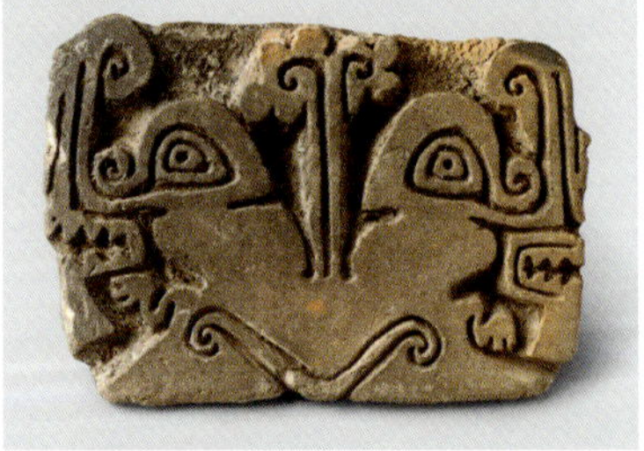

P 40

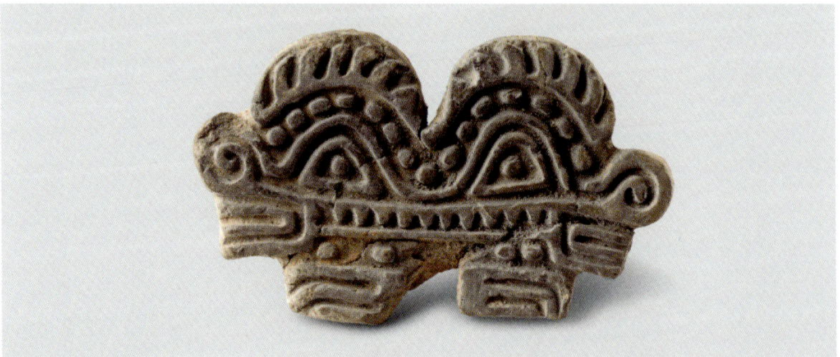

P 43

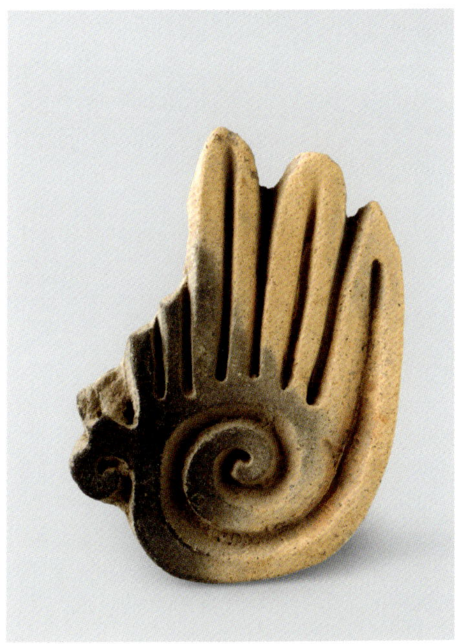

P 44

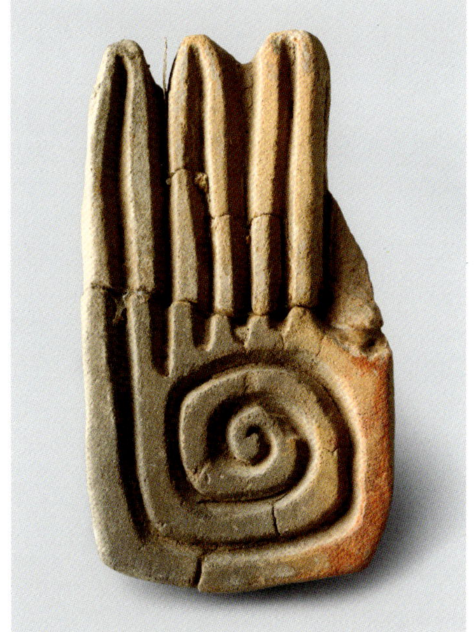

P 45

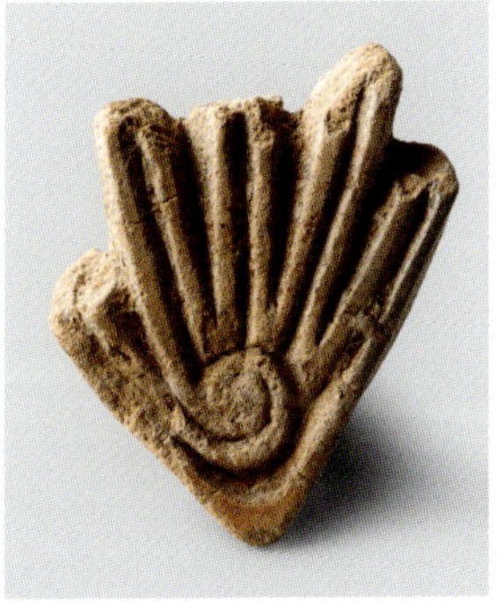

P 46

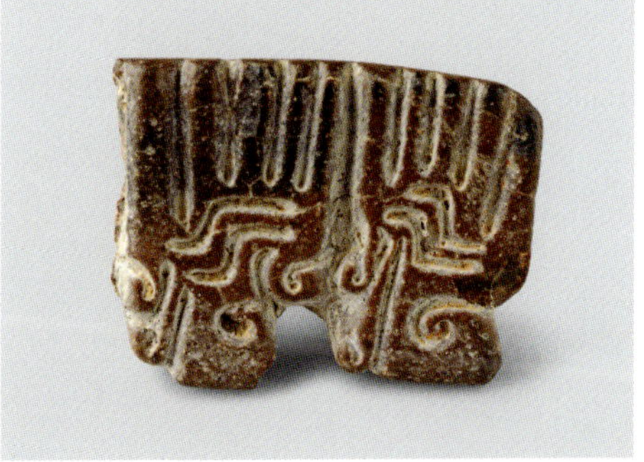

P 47

Another part of the human figure might be represented emblematically on flat *sellos*: the open hand, with the five fingers growing out of a spiral that also forms the palm (**figs. P 45–P 46**) – *ojo en mano*, as one scholar defines it[103] – opening out to the surrounding area; we may even have both hands (**fig. P 47**) in a centrifugal movement. The representation of a hand with a spiral on the palm is most definitively an expression of the magnetically vital energy that it traditionally emits, as exemplified in a variety of cultures.

Final Considerations

New discoveries constantly yield revisions, developments and modernizations of interpretative theories. The wide-ranging nature of Pre-Columbian *sellos*, both flat and cylindrical – here exemplified in a collection from Ecuador – proffers many different aspects. As long as we refrain from relying on other or further evidence, however, or at least on substantive clues, uncertainties are bound to linger. The product of unknown artists, the *sellos* provide us with mute testimony of a lost world: the many enigmas related to their fabrication and use continue to enthral us.

The purpose of the present study has been, in the first instance, to contribute to an enhanced awareness and understanding of such objects; we have compared a number of patterns and forms found in *sellos* without the least attempt at setting out definitive conclusions. Our intent has, rather, been to provide scholars with unpublished material and data they could make use of for their analysis, hoping that many other similar Pre-Columbian finds may be researched. However, despite the lack of definitive evidence, the hypothesis that attributes to the *sellos* a symbolic value as amulets or ritual objects or a form of communication should not be discounted.

One hopes that an increase in the number of similar studies might some day yield the true meaning(s) of the *sellos*. New information will undoubtedly change not only the knowledge we have acquired to date, but possibly also our understanding of the past history of these civilisations.

[63] Enciso 1947.

[64] Franch 1958.

[65] Field F.V. 1967 and 1974.

[66] Ladron 2004.

[67] Gonzales 1993, p. 95.

[68] Venturoli 2006, p. 31.

[69] *Ecuador* 1992, p. 31.

[70] Gonzales 1993, p. 54.

[71] Lathrap 1975, p. 106, fig. 526.

[72] Venturoli 2006, pp. 34, 86–91.

[73] Jorge Enciso on the other hand attributes to S, in so far as it concerns Meso-American cultures, the value of "*signo Xonecuilli (Gusano Azul), simbolo de one constelación o el Cetro de Quetzalcoatl:* (Enciso 1947, plates 55–60). It seems assured that use has been made of it for the stylisation of the serpent shape.

[74] Cummins & Burgos 1996, p. 196, fig. 107b, 197 fig. 108a/b.

[75] Gonzales 1993, p. 114.

[76] Parducci 1966, p. 124.

[77] Bodenhorst 1984, p. 43, fig. P-20.

[78] A peculiarity of this *sello* is that it might be read both as positive and negative (see reproductions).

[79] Gonzales 1993, p. 105.

[80] Gonzales 1993, p. 104.

[81] Cummins & Burgos 1996, p. 142, fig. 55a.

[82] D'Harcourt 1947, p. 92, fig. 3.

[83] Cummins & Burgos 1996, p. 146, fig. 59.

[84] Cummins & Burgos 1996, p. 144, fig. 57b.

[85] Bodenhorst 1984, pp. 46–47, fig. C-29, C-30, C-31; Cummins & Burgos 1996, p. 139, fig. 52, p. 140, fig. 53a-b, p. 141, fig. 54, p. 143, fig. 56, p. 145, fig. 58b, p. 149, fig. 62a; Lathrap 1975, p. 106, fig 531.

[86] Estrada 1959, p. 21, fig. 15; Machalilla B. Guangala Culture.

[87] Di Capua 1984, pp. 91–92; *Historia* 1977, p. 117.

[88] Cummins & Burgos 1996, p. 141, fig. 57°.

[89] Cummins & Burgos 1996, p. 142, fig. 55b.

[90] Parducci 1967, p. 159, lamina 2 (e).

[91] Parducci 1967, p. 159, lamina 2 (b, c, d), p. 163, lamina 4 (d).

[92] Parducci 1967, p. 161, lamina 3 (a, c, d).

[93] Cummins & Burgos 1996, p. 148, fig. 61d.

[94] Parducci 1967, p. 167, lamina 6.

[95] Parducci 1967, p. 165, lamina 5 (b, c); Field F.V. 1974, p. 127.

[96] Field F.V. 1974, p. 127.

[97] Saville 1907, plate LXXVIII, fig. 9.

[98] Cummins & Burgos 1996, p. 252, fig. 28a.

[99] Saville 1907, plate LXXVIII – 1, 2.

[100] Lathrap 1975, p. 106, fig 526; *Tesori* 1982, p. 113, fig. 500.

[101] Estrada 1959, p. 11.

[102] Anton 1977, p. 11 figure of flat *sello* stemming from Saint Andres Tuzcla, Vera Cruz, Mexico; Ladron 2004, pp. 33–34; Cummins & Burgos 1996, p. 155.

[103] Estrada 1959, inprint p. 78, *sellos* of Esmeraldas.

Bibliography

ALCINA J. 1978. *L'art Précolombien*. Paris: Éditions d'art Lucien Mazenod.

ANTON F. 1974. *Die Kunst der Goldländer. Zwischen Mexiko und Peru*. Leipzig: VEB E.A. Seemann.

ANTON F. 1977. *Alt-Amerika und seine Kunst*. Leipzig: VEB E.A. Seemann.

BADER M. 1972. "A Possible Focus of Andean Artistic Influence in Mesoamerica", in *Studies in Pre-Columbian Art and Archaeology*, 9; Dumbarton Oaks, Washington, D.C., Trustees for Harvard University.

BIONDI M. 1992 (ed.). *Antica America. Guida alla sezione America Precolombiana del Museo delle culture extraeuropee 'Dinz Rialto' a Rimini*. Florence: Ponte alle Grazie Ed.

BODENHORST B. 1984. "Los sellos cerámicos de Manabí", in *Antropologia Ecuadoriana*, 2–3, pp. 23–56; Quito, Casa de la Cultura Ecuadoriana.

CERÁMICA 1975. "Cerámica colombia-ecuador – poterie des Pays andins", in *ABC Décor*. Paris, December.

CLAY 2005. *Clay Shamans and stone Jaguars. The Ancient Art of Ecuador*. Budapest: Museum of Ethnography.

COLLON D. 1997 (ed.). *7000 Years of Seals*. London: British Museum Press.

COLOMBIEN 1975. *L'art colombien à travers les siècles*. Paris: Petit Palais, November 1975 – February 1976.

CUMMINS & BURGOS J. 1996. "Arte prehispánico del Ecuador: Huellas del Pasado. Los sellos del Jama-Coaque", in *Miscelanea Antropologica Ecuadoriana*, monograph series, 11, Guayaquil, Banco Central del Ecuador.

DE LANDA D. 1864. *Relación de las cosas de Yucatan*. Paris.

D'HARCOURT R. 1947. "Archéologie de la Province d'Esmeraldas (Equateur)", in *Journal de la Société des Américanistes,* vol XXXIV, pp. 61–200.

D'HARCOURT R. 1962. *Textiles of ancient Perú and their techniques*. Seattle: University of Washington Press.

DI CAPUA C. 1984. "Consideraciones sobre una exposición de sellos arqueológicos", in *Antropologia Ecuatoriana*, 2–3, pp. 79–103; Quito, Casa de la Cultura Ecuadoriana.

DISSELHOFF H. & LINNÉ S. 1961 *Antica America*. Milan: Il Saggiatore.

DRESDNER BANK 1989. *4000 jahre vor Kolumbus Keramik- und Steinkunst aus Ecuador*. Austellungskatalog der Dresdner Bank, Dresdner Bank ARG.

ECUADOR 1992. *Ecuador, la tierra y el oro*. exhibition catalogue, Genoa, Museo di Sant'Agostino 1992–1993. Rome: Leonardo De Luca Ed.

ENCISO J. 1947. *Sellos del Antiguo México*. México: D.F.

ESTRADA E. 1959. "Arte aborigen del Ecuador – Sellos o Pintaderas," in *Humanitas, Boletin ecuatoriano de antropologia*, pp.7–17; Quito, Editorial Universitaria.

ESTRELLA E. 1993. *La biodiversidad en el Ecuador. Historia y realidad*. Quito: Tallpa Editores.

FIELD F.V. 1967. "Thoughts on the Meaning and Use of Pre-Hispanic Mexican sellos", *Studies in Pre-Columbian Art and Archeology*, 3; Dumbarton Oaks, Washington, D.C., Trustees for Harvard University.

FIELD F.V. 1974. *Hispanic Mexican Stamp Designs*. New York: Dover Publications.

FRANCH J.A. 1958. *Las 'Pintaderas' mejicanas y sus relaciones*. Madrid: Instituto Gonzalo Fernández de Oviedo.

FUHRMANN E. 1922. *Mexico III.* Hague-Darmstadt: Folkwang Verlag.

GHEORGHIU D. & SKEATES R. 2008. *Prehistoric Stamps, Theory and Experiments*. Bucharest: Editura universitātii din Bucuresti.

GONZÁLES F. 1993. *I simboli precolombiani*. Rome: Ed. Mediterranée.

GUÉNON R. 1987. *Considerazioni sulla via iniziatica*. Genoa: Melita Ed.

HISTORIA 1977. *Historia del Arte Ecuatoriano*. vol. I fasc.18, p. 117, Barcelona: Salvat Editores.

KLEIN D. & CEVALLOS I. 2007. *Ecuador. The Secret Art of Precolumbian Ecuador*. Milan: Five Continents Ed.

KUBLER G. 1967. "The Iconography of the Art of Teotihuacán" in *Studies in Pre-Columbian Art and Archeology*, 4, pp. 3–40; Dumbarton Oaks, Washington, D.C., Trustees for Harvard University.

LADRON DE GUEVARA S. 2004. *Diseños precolombinos de Vera Cruz*. Veracruz: Editora de Gobierno.

LAPINER A. 1976. *Pre-Columbian Art of South America*. New York: Harry N. Abrams.

LATHRAP D.W. 1975. *Ancient Ecuador, Culture, Clay and Creativity, 3000–300 B.C.* Chicago: Field Museum of Natural History.

LAURENCICH-MINNELLI L. 1983. *Messico precolombiano. Testimonianze per un'indagine archeologica e storica*. Bologna: Soc. Ed. Esculapio.

LÉVI-STRAUSS C. 2002. *Mito e significato*. Milan: Net.

MASON J.A. 1961. *Le antiche civiltà del Perù*. Florence: Sansoni.

MAYA 1998. *I Maya,* exhibition catalogue, Venice. Milan: Bompiani.

MEGGERS B.J. 1966. *Ecuador (Ancient Peoples and Places)*. London: Thames and Hudson.

MUSEO 1966. *Museo Nacional del Banco Central del Ecuador, Sala de Arqueología*, catalogue, Quito.

ORTEGON A. 1999. *Pre-Columbian Stamp Seals.* Pueblo: AOA Associates.

PARDUCCI R.Z. 1961. "Representacion de Casas en los Sellos Triangulares de Manabí", in *Cuadernos de Historia y Arqueologia*, vol. X, 27, pp. 231–242; Guayaquil, Casa de la Cultura Ecuadoriana, Núcleo del Guayas.

PARDUCCI R.Z. 1966. "Sellos zoomorfos de Manabì, Ecuador" in *Cuadernos de Historia y Arqueologia*, 28–29, pp. 123–135; Guayaquil, Casa de la Cultura Ecuadoriana, Núcleo del Guayas.

PARDUCCI R.Z. 1967. "Sellos Antropomorfos de Manabí, Ecuador", in *Cuadernos de Historia y Arqueologia*, 33, XVII, pp.143–167; Guayaquil, Casa de la Cultura Ecuadoriana, Núcleo del Guayas.

PERU 2003. *Perù. Tremila anni di capolavori.* exhibition catalogue, Florence. Milan: Electa.

RESTREPO M. 1992. "Valores culturales de Tierradentro", in *Cuadernos de Tierradentro,* 1, Istituto Colombiano de Antropologia.

RICCHIERI G. 2002. *La cultura tumaco-tolita.* Bologna: Editrice Missionaria Italiana.

SALOMONE G.D. 1975. *10.000 anni di arte precolombiana.* Milan: Antonio Cordani Ed.

SAVILLE M.H. 1907. *The Antiquities of Manabí, Ecuador.* 2 vols., New York.

SCHAFFER F.W. 1979. *Indian Designs from ancient Ecuador.* New York: Dover Publications.

SELLOS 1982. *Sellos o Pintaderas Precolombinas de la Costa Ecuadoriana.* exhibition catalogue, Museo Arqueologico del Banco del Pacifico, Guayaquil 1982.

SOTHEBY'S 1989. Sotheby's, *Auction Catalogue.* November 20, 40, New York.

SOTHEBY'S 1992. Sotheby's, *Auction Catalogue.* November 23, New York.

SOTHEBY'S 1994. Sotheby's, *Auction Catalogue.* November 15, New York.

SOUSTELLE J. 1995. *Olmechi. La più antica civiltà del Messico.* Florence: Rusconi Ed.

TESORI 1982. *I tesori della terra di Atahualpa – Ecuador dalla preistoria agli Inca.* exhibition catalogue, Venice. Venice: Marsilio.

TESORI 1982. *I tesori della terra di Atahualpa – Ecuador dalla preistoria agli Inca.* exhibition catalogue, Locarno, BSI banca della svizzera italiana.

TESORI 2004. *I tesori degli aztechi.* exhibition catalogue, Rome. Milan: Electa.

TOTEN 1999. *Vom Toten Meer zum Stillen Ozean.* Ostfildern-Ruit: Verlag Gert Hatje.

TRÉSORS 1974. *Trésors de l'Equateur.* exhibition catalogue, Musée d'Ethnographie de Genève, Geneva.

VALDEZ F. & VEINTIMILLA D. 1992. *Signos amerindios. 5000 años de arte precolombino en Ecuador.* Paris: Ediciones Colibrí.

VENTUROLI S. 2006. *Le religioni dell'antico Perù.* Rome: Carocci Ed.

VERNAU R. & RIVET P. 1922. *Éthnographie anciennne de l'Equateur.* Paris: Premier Fascicule, 1912, Deuxième Fascicule, 1922.

VILLÈLIA M. 2006. *Quitu-Cara, una cultura entre els dos hemisferis. Exposició.* Girona: Fundació Caixa Girona.

VON HAGEN. 1977. *Civiltà e splendore degli aztechi,* Rome: Newton Compton Ed.

WILBERT J. 1974. "The Thread of Life. Symbolism of Miniature Art from Ecuador", in *Studies in Pre-Columbian Art and Archaelogy*, 12, Dumbarton Oaks, Washington, D.C., Trustees for Harvard University.

ZANETTI G. 1992 (ed.). *Prima dell'America. 4000 anni di arte precolombiana.* exhibition catalogue, Prima, Bologna. Museo Archeologico, Bologna, Milan: Silvana editoriale.

ZANETTI G. 1995. "Sellos e pintaderas precolombiani", in Euro Capellini 1995 (ed.) *Il sigillo, impronta dell'uomo,* pp. 114–116; Milan: Mondadori.

All objects are in various private collections.

All measurements are expressed in millimeters; dimensions (h × l × d).

The thermoluminescence tests (TLT) that were carried out on the *sellos* listed below show dates that are more recent than those currently found in the traditional chronologies of ancient cultures of Ecuador (TLTs were all carried out at the Ralf Kotalla laboratory in Haigerloch, Germany). This would *seem* to suggest that these cultures have survived longer than generally assumed. All values of TLTs are to be taken as +/– 20%.

Catalogue Flat Sellos

P 1

Culture: Manteña

Dimensions: 25 × 18 × 22

TLT: - 560 years

Object description: greyish, convex terracotta with cone-shaped handle at the back

Iconography: frontally positioned figure wearing a plumed headdress

Condition: intact

Bibl. ref.: Parducci 1967, plate 5

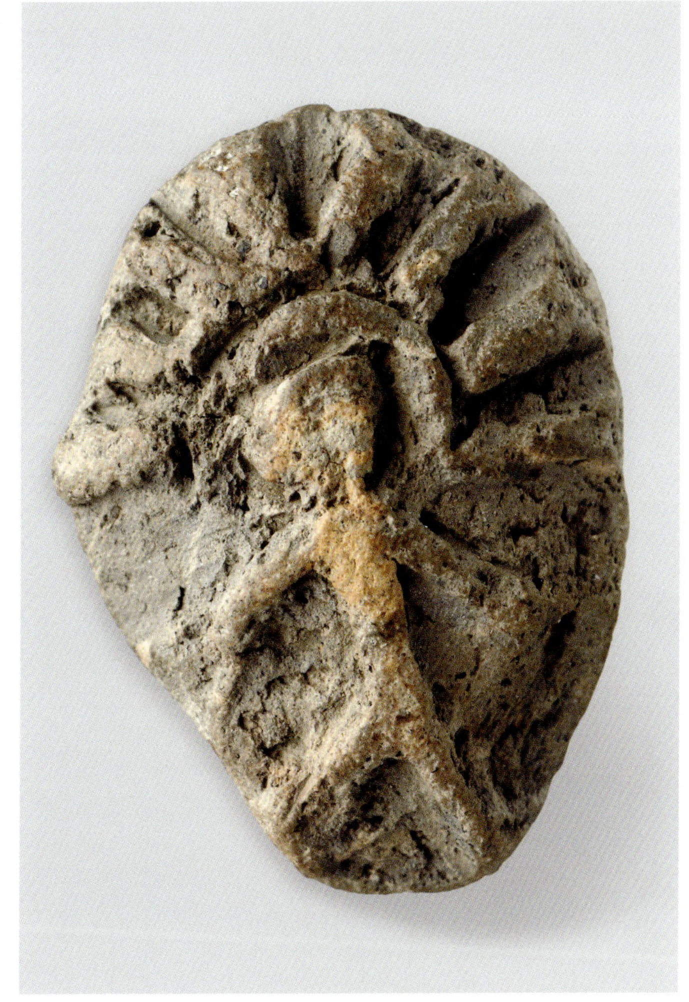

P 2

Culture: uncertain

Dimensions: 65 × 37 × 37

TLT: not available

Object description: flat brownish terracotta with cone-shaped handle at the back

Iconography: stylised frontal figure with arms in 'praying' position and legs wide apart. The head features a plume of rays and the stomach is protruding

Condition: handle at the back is broken and has been glued to the main body. Small elements are missing

Prov.: Gerhard Hirsch Estate, Munich (D), Auction 257, 23–24 September 2008

P 3

Culture: Manteña

Dimensions: 20 × 35 × 30

TLT: not available

Object description: central fragment of a flat *sello* made of brown-greyish terracotta with cone-shaped handle at the back

Iconography: stylised crouching figure in 'praying' position flanked by patterns of radiating suns

Condition: central part of *sello* only: two sides are missing

Prov.: Gerhard Hirsch Estate, Munich (D), Auction 257, 23–24 September 2008

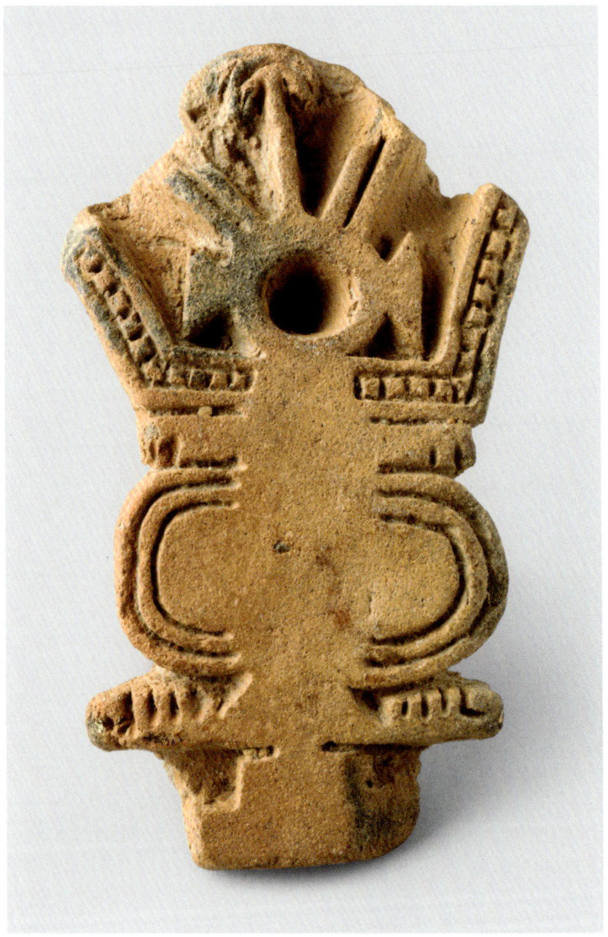

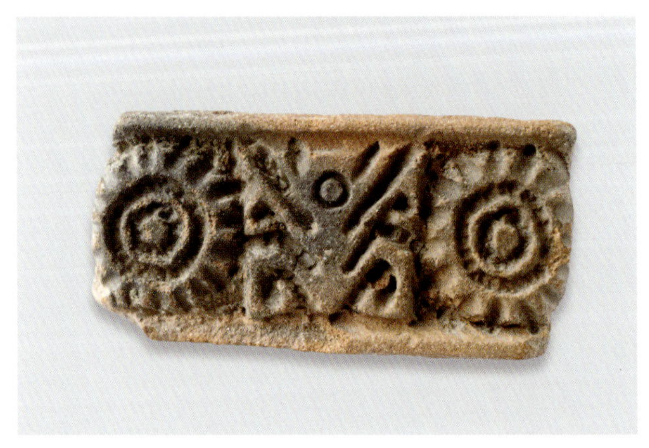

P 4

Culture: Jama-Coaque

Dimensions: 91 × 47 × 43

TLT: not available

Object description: flat brown terracotta with greyish shadings, with cone-shaped handle at the back

Iconography: stylised frontal figure with feet wide apart. Two points on each foot indicate toes (which might otherwise be taken to be serpent heads). The head is surrounded by a plume of rays, and the whole figure is surrounded by clouds

Condition: some corner parts are missing and the fractured parts have been glued

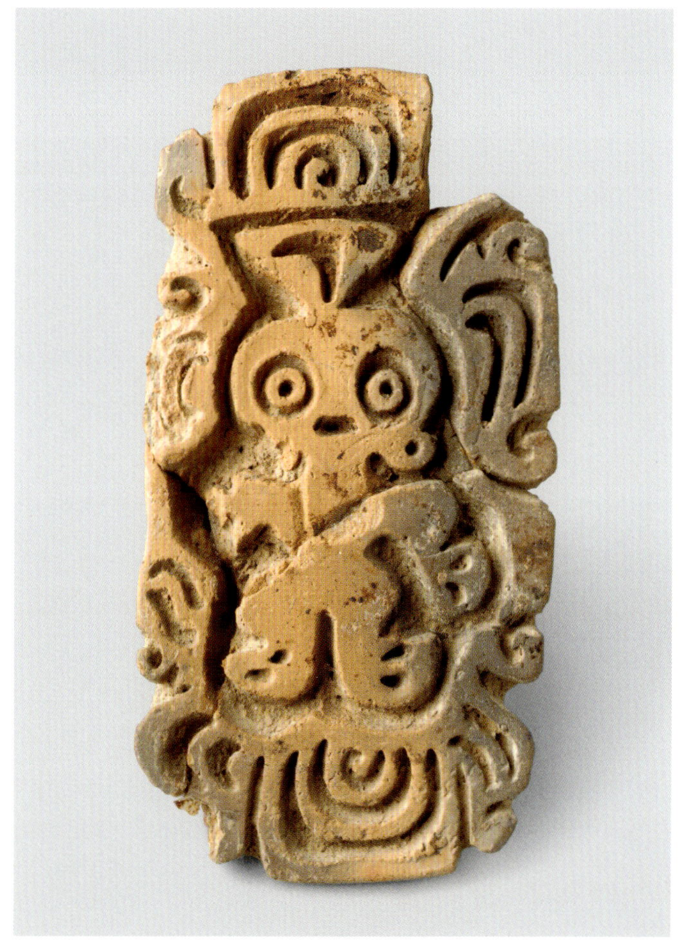

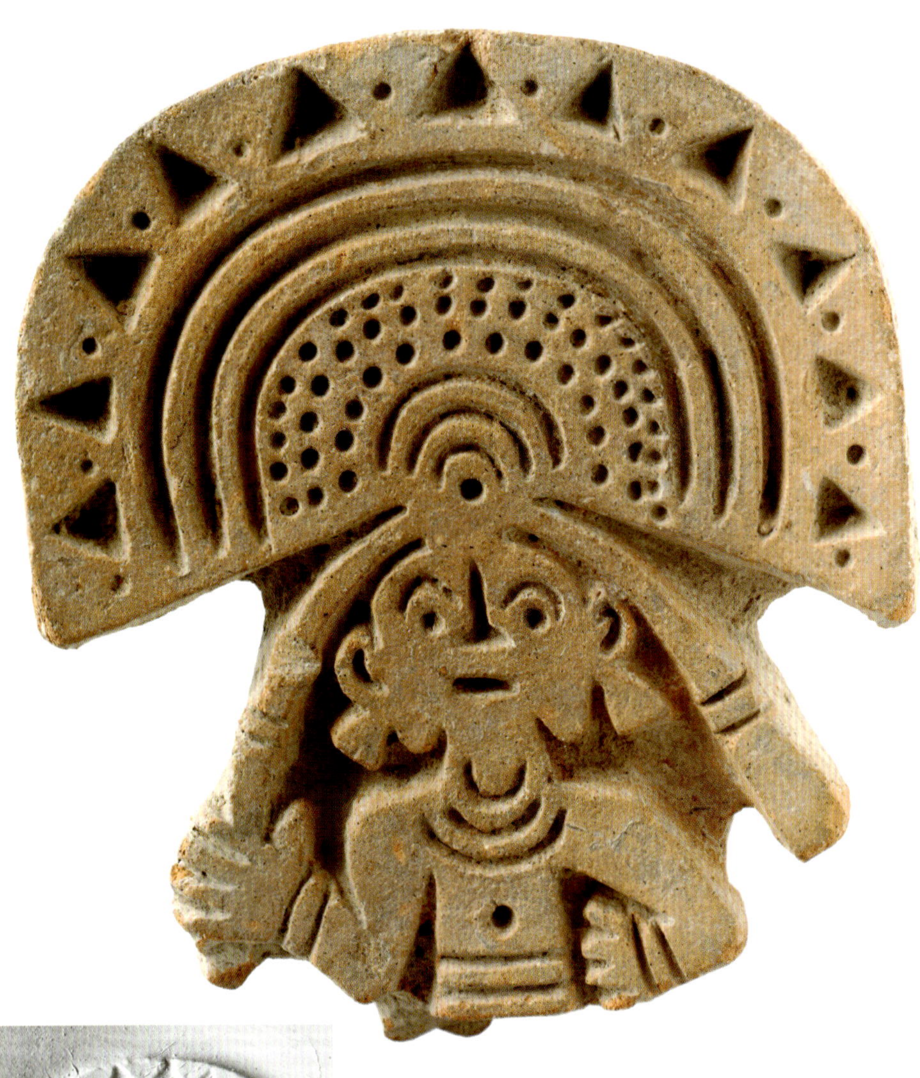

P 5 (left)

Culture: late Jama-Coaque

Dimensions: 65 × 56 × 47

TLT: - 1200 years

Object description: flat brownish terracotta with a cone-shaped handle at the back

Iconography: frontal figure with wide plumed hat and wearing a necklace

Condition: the lower part of the handle is missing

Ref.: Museo de las Culturas Aborigenes, Cuenca, Ecuador – Guia: Hall no. 8, Esculturilla Danzante Jama-Coaque

Prov.: Argentum, Juan Leon Mera 614 Quito, purchased 1995

P 6

Culture: Jama-Coaque

Dimensions: 35 × 70 × 15

TLT: not available

Object description: flat brownish terracotta with cone-shaped handle at the back. Slight convexity

Iconography: double bands divide *sello* centrally into two vertical tiers. The left tier shows a sequence of superimposed stylised figures. The masked head is shown in profile facing left, while the body is placed frontally. The right-adjacent tier shows masks placed horizontally in reverse pattern between mirrored diagonal bands. The tier is banded at the right edge

Condition: central part of *sello* only: two sides and the handle are missing

Bibl. ref.: Saville 1907

Prov.: Gerhard Hirsch Estate, Munich (D), Auction 257, 23–24 September 2008

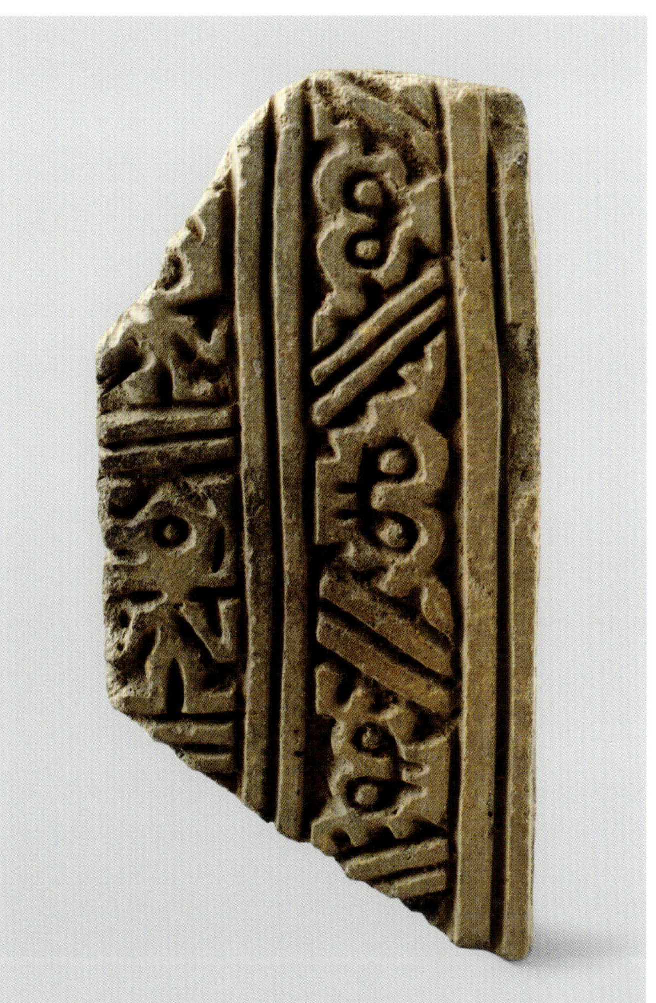

Culture: Manteña

Dimensions: 34 × 26 × 34

TLT: not available

Object description: flat dark terracotta with cone-shaped handle at the back

Iconography: masked, tailed figure. Legs and head are shown in profile facing left; the trunk is placed frontally and shows a necklace. Both arms are folded overhead

Condition: intact

Prov.: Gerhard Hirsch Estate, Munich (D), Auction 257, 23–24 September 2008

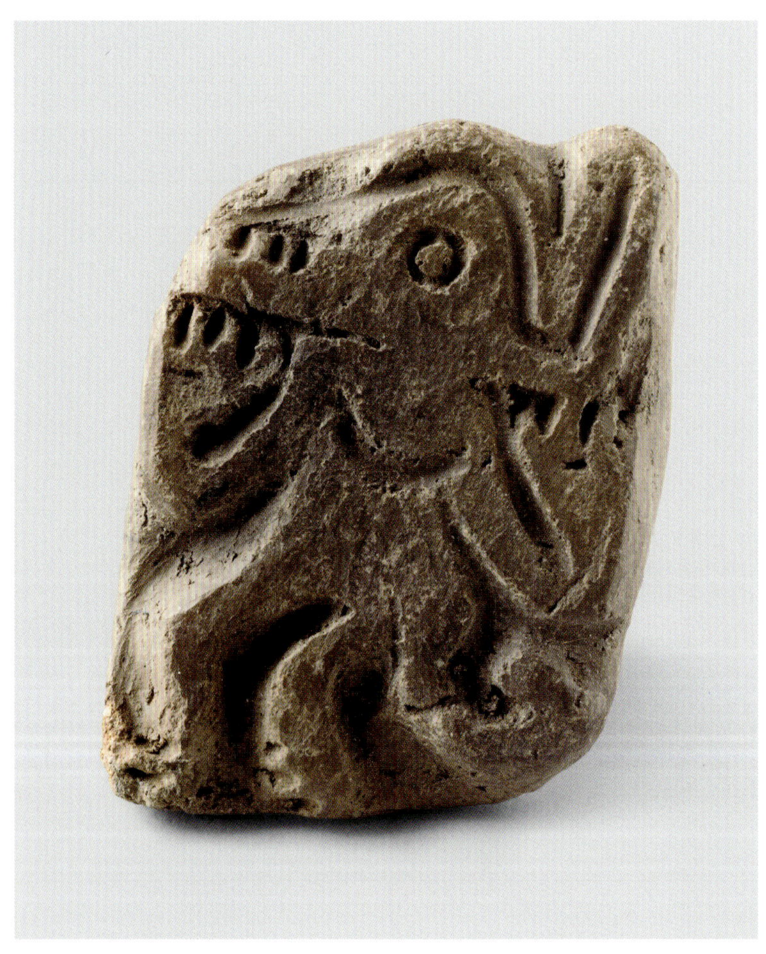

Culture: Manteña

Dimensions: 40 × 26 × 38

TLT: not available

Object description: flat greyish terracotta with cone-shaped handle at the back

Iconography: masked figure whose head is shown in profile facing right, while legs and trunk are placed frontally; arms are held open

Condition: intact, but figure shows signs of wear

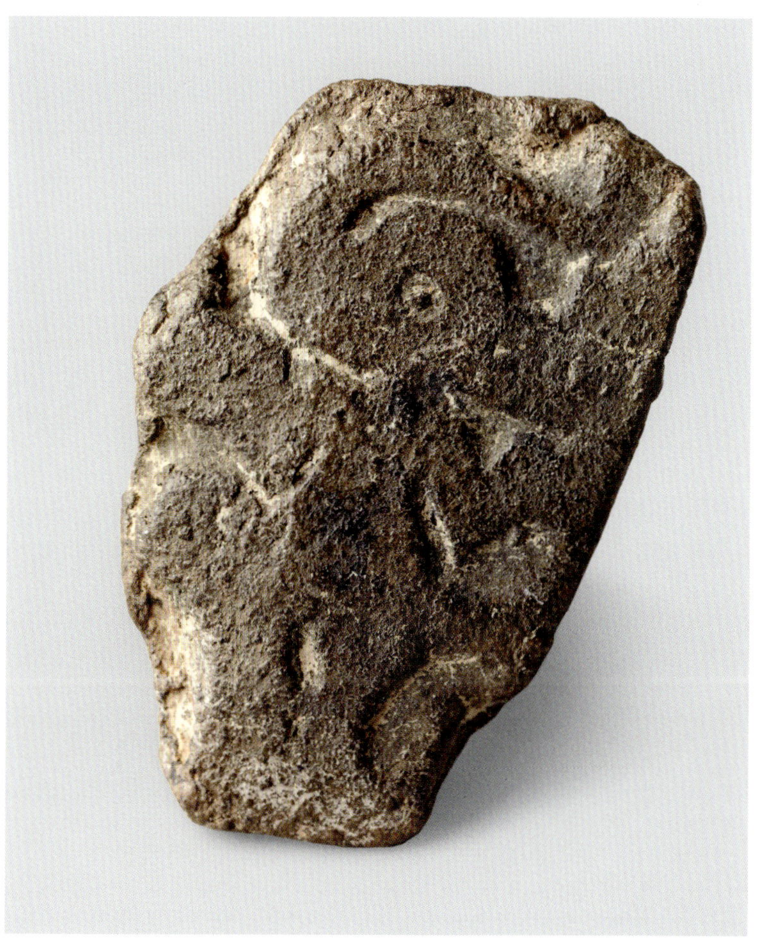

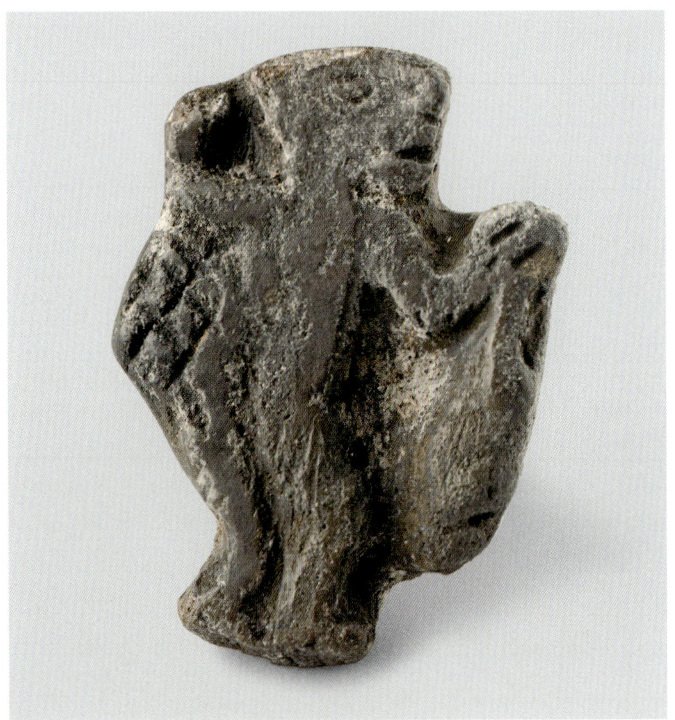

P 9

Culture: Manteña

Dimensions: 37 × 26 × 36

TLT: not available

Object description: flat black terracotta with cone-shaped handle at the back

Iconography: anthropomorphic figure with both head and legs shown in profile facing right; chest and arms are frontal. Objects are in the left hand and on the shoulder

Condition: intact, but figure shows signs of wear

Bibl. ref.: Parducci 1967, plate 4 c-d

Prov.: Gerhard Hirsch Estate, Munich (D), Auction 257, 23–24 September 2008

P 10 (right)

Culture: Manteña

Dimensions: 68 × 30 × 31

TLT: not available

Object description: flat greyish terracotta with cone-shaped handle at the back

Iconography: masked standing figure with wide plumed helmet. Head and legs are shown in profile facing right, trunk is frontal with visible male genitals. Arms are held open and hold two staffs, one of which shows a crossed and dotted rhombus

Condition: intact

Bibl. ref.: Parducci 1967, plate 4 d

Prov.: Gerhard Hirsch Estate, Munich (D), Auction 257, 23–24 September 2008

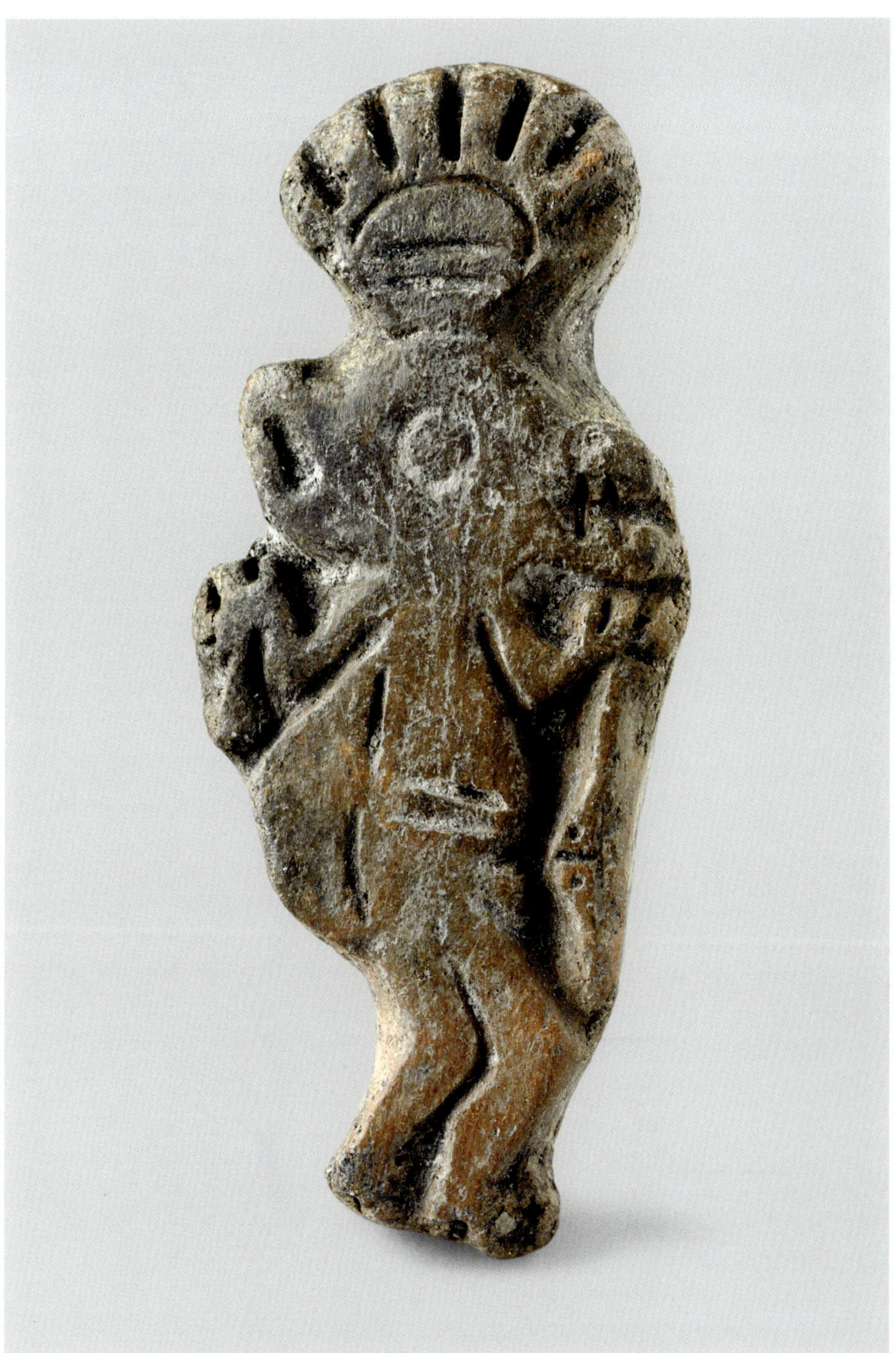

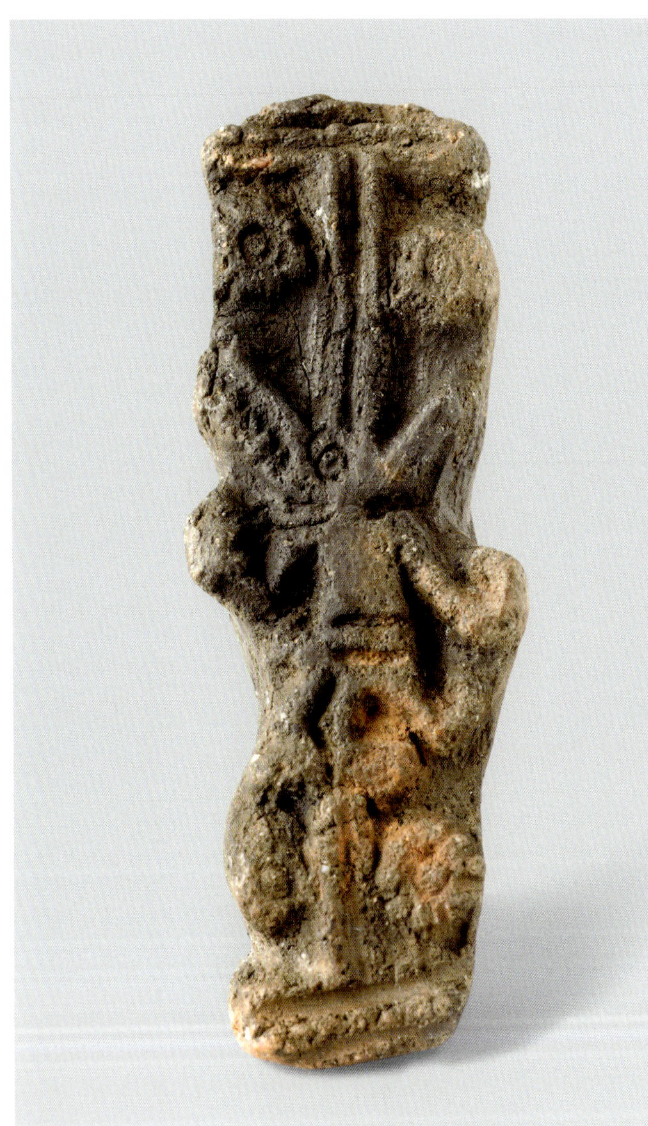

P 11

Culture: Manteña

Dimensions: 50 × 20 × 40

TLT: not available

Object description: flat brown-greyish terracotta with cone-shaped handle at the back

Iconography: anthropomorphic masked figure shown in profile facing left. Above and underneath are two mirrored patterns radiating from the centre. They are connected with a T-shaped grooved pattern enclosing floral or sun-like patterns

Condition: intact, but figure shows signs of wear

Prov.: Gerhard Hirsch Estate, Munich (D), Auction 257, 23–24 September 2008

P 12 (right)

Culture: Manteña

Dimensions: 55 × 48 × 38

TLT: not available

Object description: flat greyish terracotta with cone-shaped handle at the back

Iconography: masked figure with tail, standing with open arms and holding two staffs. Image is shown in profile facing right with visible male genitals, inside a square frame

Condition: intact

Prov.: Gerhard Hirsch Estate, Munich (D), Auction 257, 23–24 September 2008

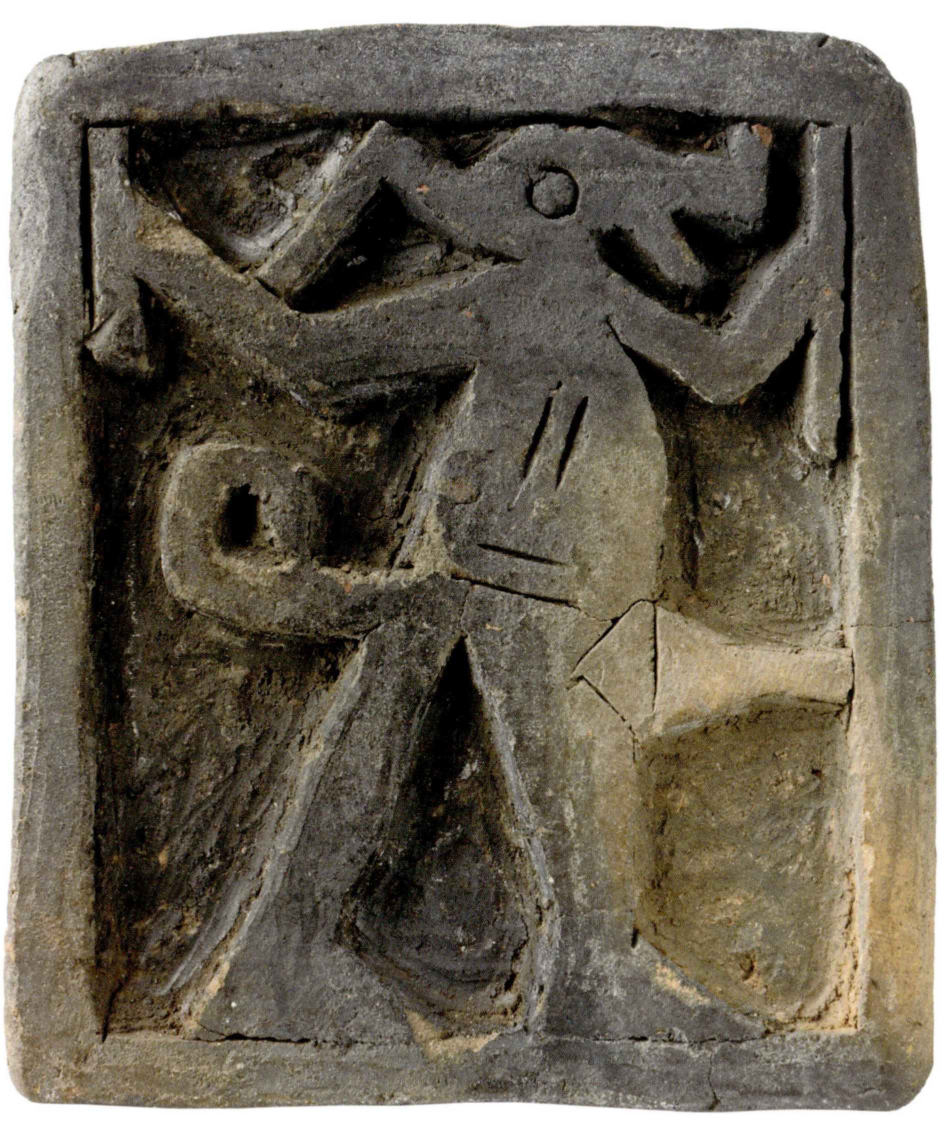

Culture: Manteña

Dimensions: 61.5 × 50 × 43

TLT: not available

Object description: flat greyish terracotta with cone-shaped handle at the back

Iconography: stylised tailed figure with masked head shown in profile facing right and bearing a plumed helmet. The body is shown frontally wearing a necklace or collar. Feet are shown laterally. It holds an analogous (probably female) figure wearing a mask which faces to the right

Condition: incomplete, figure shows signs of wear

Bibl. ref.: Parducci 1967, plate 1 a

Prov.: Gerhard Hirsch Estate, Munich (D), Auction 257, 23–24 September 2008

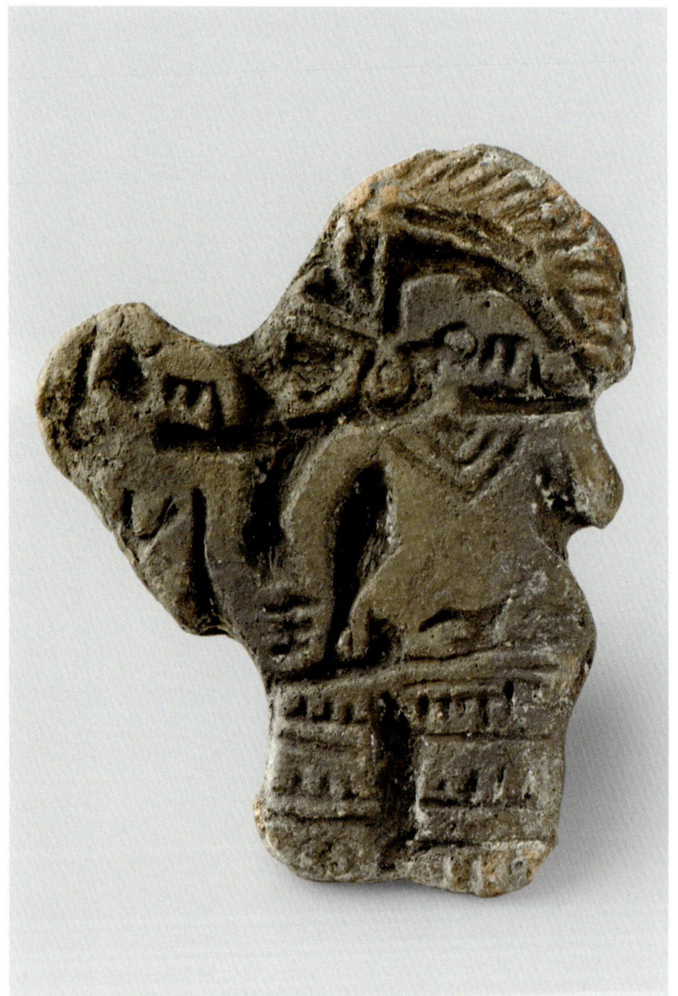

Culture: Manteña

Dimensions: 57 × 42 × 27

TLT: not available

Object description: flat greyish terracotta with cone-shaped handle at the back

Iconography: standing figure wearing elaborate plumed headdress. Legs and male genitals are shown in profile facing right, chest is frontal with necklace and belt. It holds in the left hand some sort of harpoon with a rhombic dotted insert

Condition: intact

Bibl. ref.: an equivalent figure is found in Anton 1974, p. 72; Anton 1977, p. 87; Parducci 1967, plate 2 b-d and 4 d; Wilbert 1974, p. 67, fig. 77 as part of flat *sello* that includes three other zoomorphic figures

Prov.: Gerhard Hirsch Estate, Munich (D), Auction 257, 23–24 September 2008

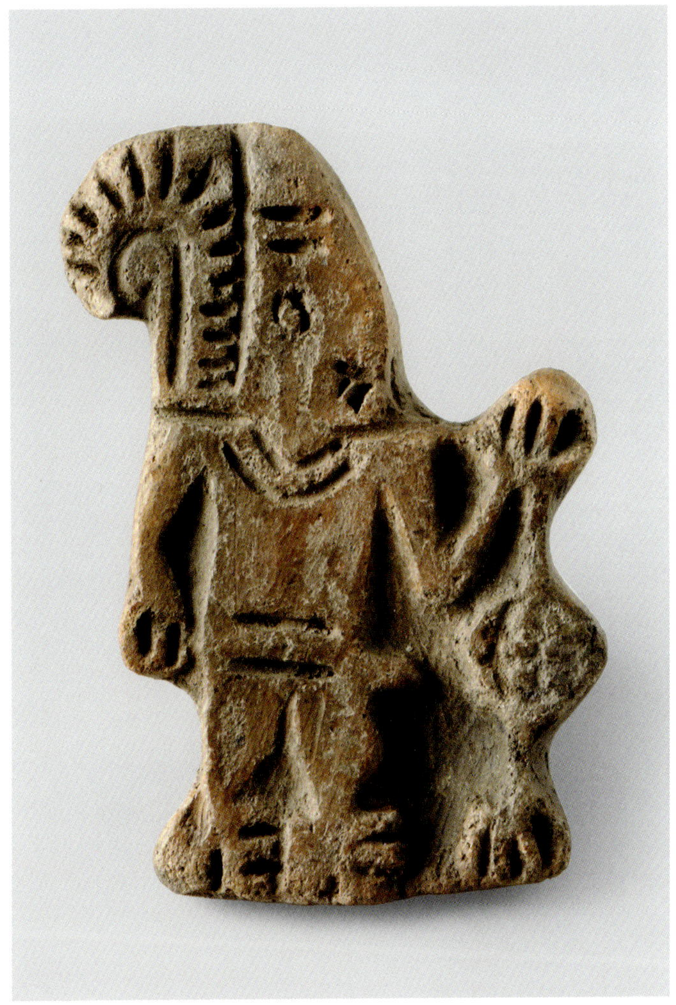

P 15

Culture: Manteña

Dimensions: 33 × 43 × 36

TLT: not available

Object description: flat greyish terracotta with cone-shaped handle at the back

Iconography: masked standing figure shown in profile facing left and holding with both hands a staff with a trophy on its tip

Condition: intact

Bibl ref.: Parducci 1967, plate 3 a, c

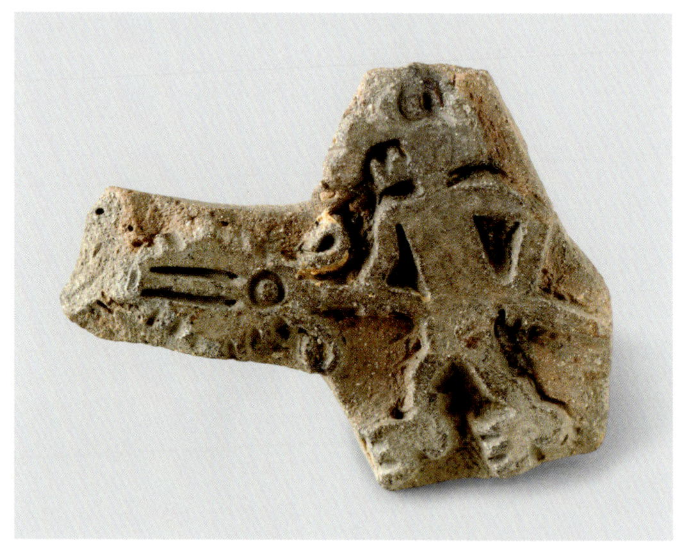

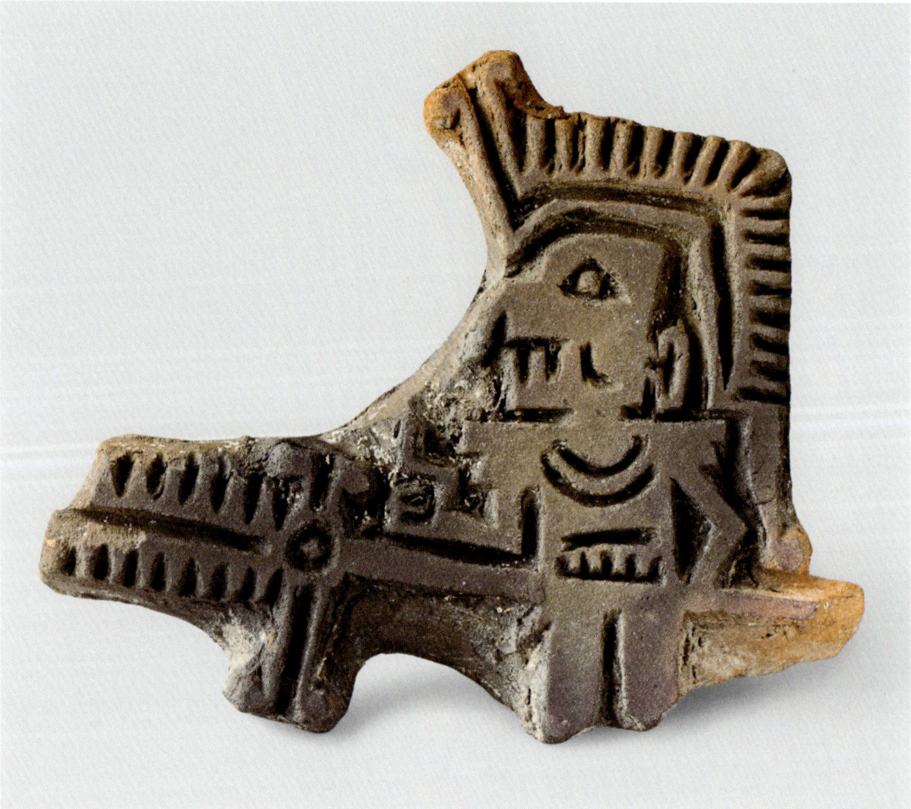

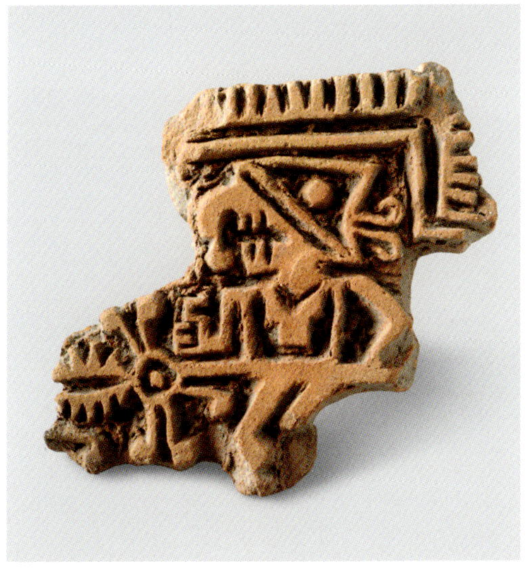 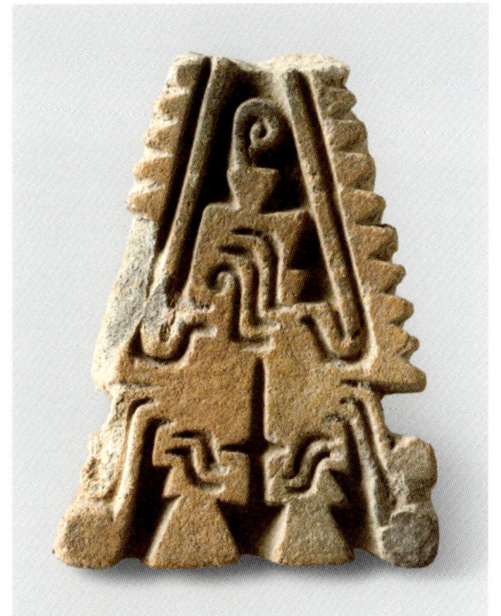

P 16 (below left)

Culture: Manteña

Dimensions: 73 × 90 × 49

TLT: not available

Object description: flat greyish terracotta with cone-shaped handle at the back

Iconography: stylised standing figure with head shown in profile facing left. It wears a wide plumed helmet. The body is shown frontally, with shoulder pads, necklaces and loincloth. Shape holds a staff in its left hand with a trophy on its tip

Condition: sections of the lower part might be missing. Probable later ink stains

Bibl. ref.: Parducci 1967, plate 3 a, c

Prov.: Gerhard Hirsch Estate, Munich (D) , Auction 257, 23–24 September 2008

P 17

Culture: Manteña

Dimensions: 40 × 46 × 27

TLT: not available

Object description: flat reddish terracotta with cone-shaped handle at the back

Iconography: stylised standing figure, masked with head shown in profile facing left. It wears a wide plumed helmet. The body is shown frontally wearing a necklace. Shape holds a staff in its left hand with a trophy on its tip

Condition: incomplete

Bibl. ref.: Parducci 1967, plate 3 a, c

Prov.: Gerhard Hirsch Estate, Munich (D), Auction 257, 23–24 September 2008

P 18

Culture: Jama-Coaque

Dimensions: 45 × 35 × 48

TLT: not available

Object description: flat brown terracotta with greyish shadings, with cone-shaped handle at the back

Iconography: stylised pattern of a figure (?) encased in triangular profile

Condition: the upper part is missing

Bibl. ref.: Cummins & Burgos 1996, p. 148, fig. 61d

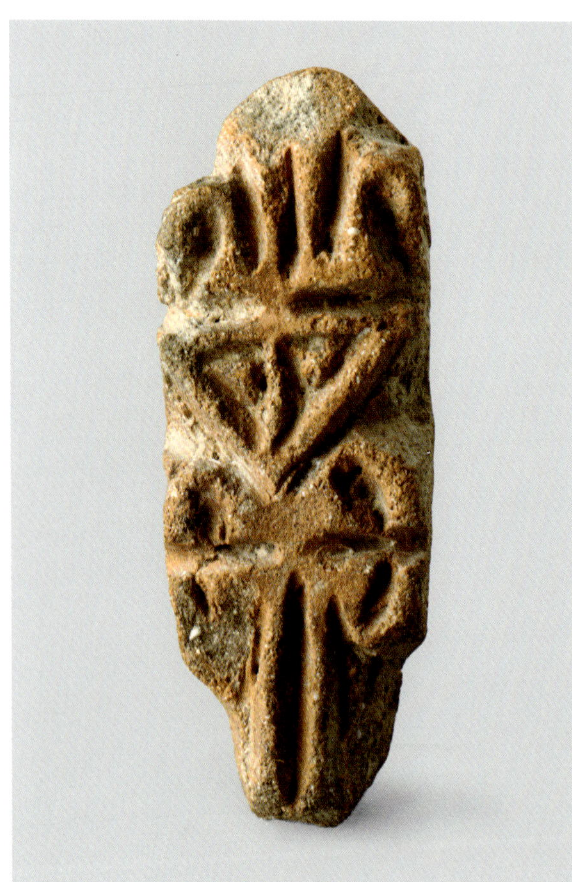

P 19

Culture: Manteña

Dimensions: 31 × 11.5 × 26

TLT: not available

Object description: flat brownish terracotta with cone-shaped handle at the back

Iconography: stylised plumed figure shown frontally

Condition: small element of the upper part is missing

Bibl. ref.: Parducci 1967, plate 6 a, f, h

P 20 (right)

Culture: Manteña

Dimensions: 37 × 13 × 28

TLT: not available

Object description: flat reddish terracotta with cone-shaped handle at the back

Iconography: stylised plumed figure shown frontally. When reversed, anthropomorphic masked figures may be detected

Condition: elements of the lower part are missing

Bibl. ref.: Parducci 1967, plate 6 b

78

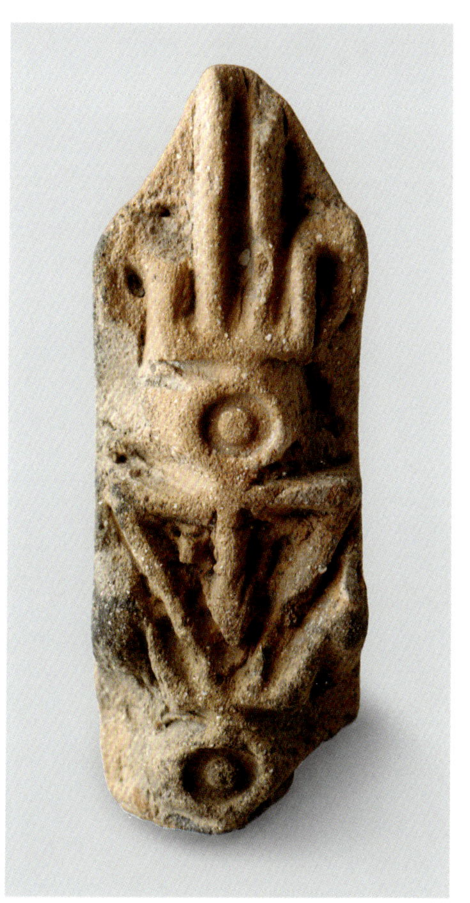 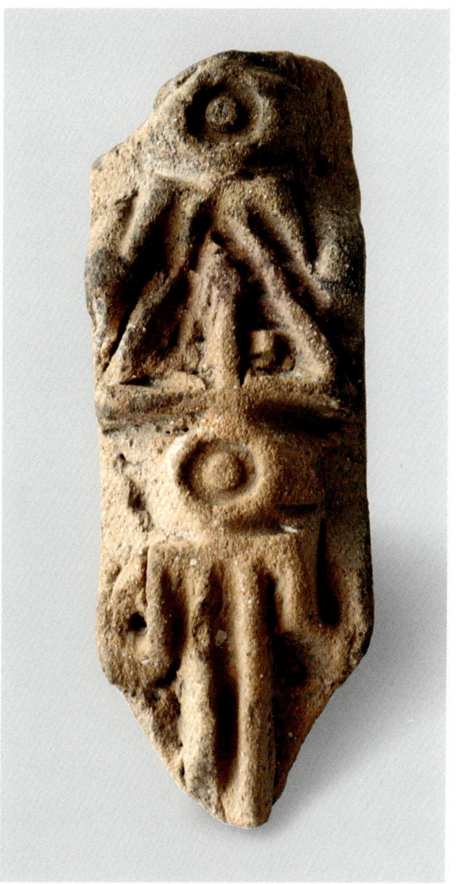

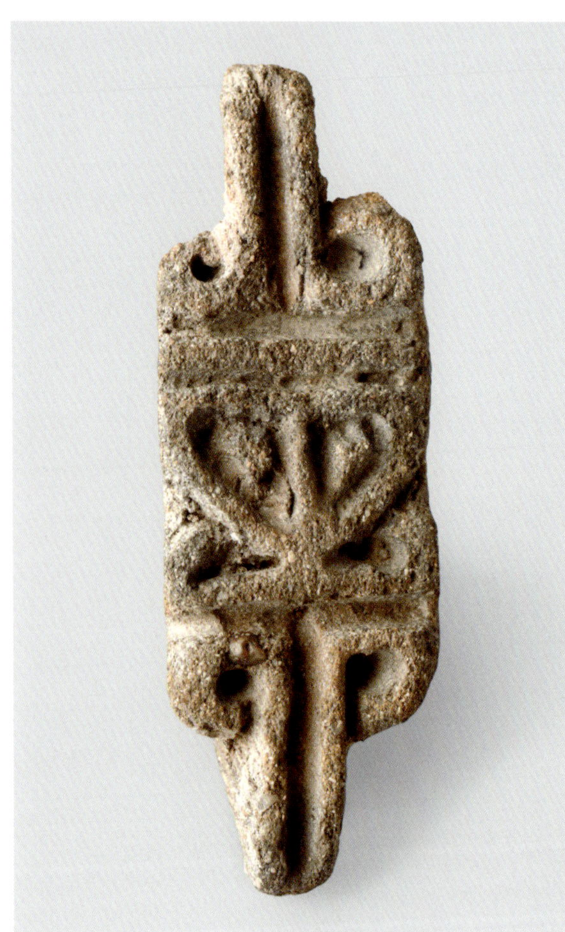

P 21

Culture: Manteña

Dimensions: 36 × 12 × 24

TLT: not available

Object description: flat greyish terracotta with cone-shaped handle at the back

Iconography: stylised, anthropomorphic plumed figure shown frontally

Condition: intact

Bibl. ref.: Parducci 1967, plate 6 a, f, h

Prov.: Gerhard Hirsch Estate, Munich (D), Auction 257, 23–24 September 2008

P 22 (right)

Culture: Manteña

Dimensions: 30 × 10 × 30

TLT: not available

Object description: flat brownish terracotta with cone-shaped handle at the back

Iconography: stylised plumed figure shown frontally. Possibly to be read in either direction

Condition: small element is missing

Bibl. ref.: Parducci 1967, plate 6 a, f, h

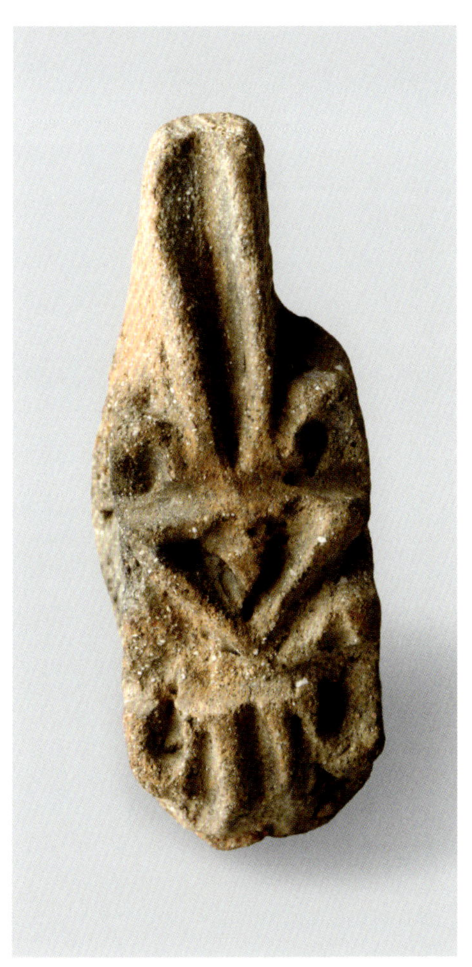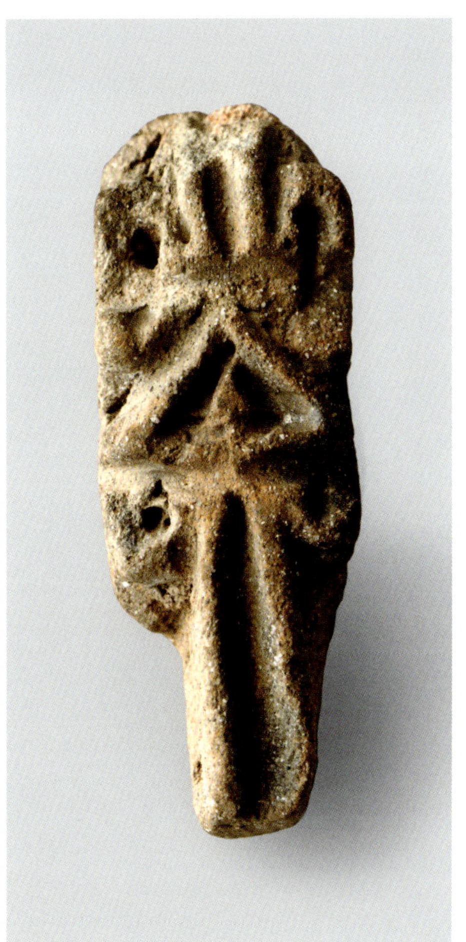

P 23

Culture: Manteña

Dimensions: 3.9 × 11 × 24

TLT: - 540 years

Object description: flat reddish terracotta with cone-shaped handle at the back

Iconography: stylised plumed figure shown frontally. Limbs are turned outward. Possibly to be read in either direction

Condition: intact

Bibl. ref.: Parducci 1967, plate 6 a, f, h

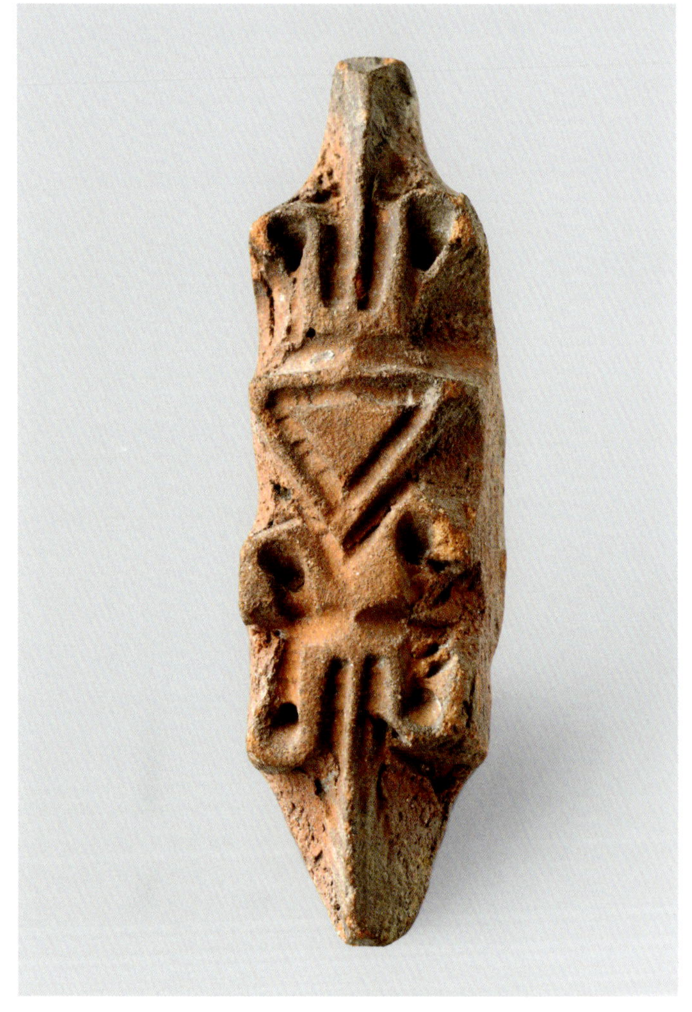

P 24

Culture: Manteña

Dimensions: 26.5 × 25 × 39

TLT: not available

Object description: flat black terracotta with cone-shaped handle at the back

Iconography: stylised face wearing plumes. Possibly to be read in either direction

Condition: intact

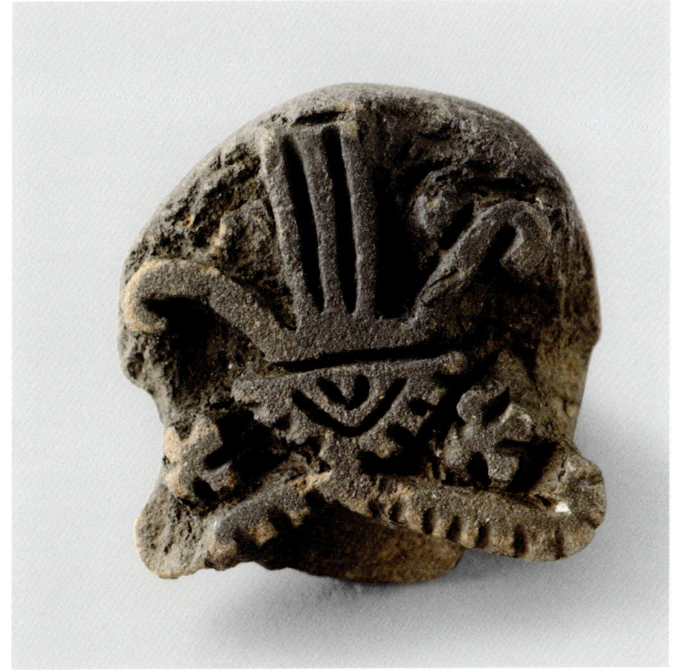

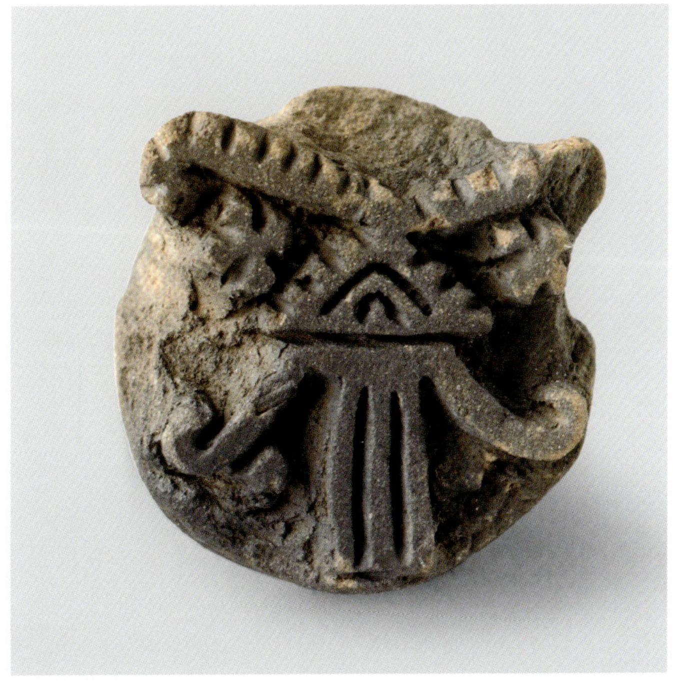

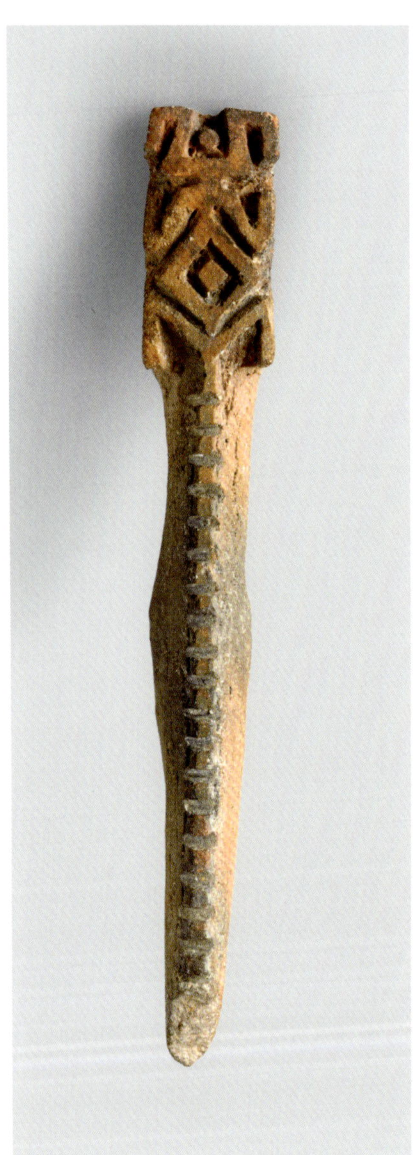

P 25

Culture: Manteña

Dimensions: 74 × 11 × 29

TLT: not available

Object description: flat reddish terracotta with greyish shadings, with cone-shaped handle at the back

Iconography: stylised figure with ventral rhombus above a series of dots

Condition: elements of the lower part are missing

P 26 (right)

Culture: Jama-Coaque

Dimensions: 79 × 67 × 61

TLT: not available

Object description: flat brownish terracotta with cone-shaped handle at the back

Iconography: along the major diagonal of two central lozenges two stylised mirrored faces prolonged as staffs. On the side are two mirrored stylised figures as well as S-shaped patterns ending in plumes

Condition: handle is glued

Bibl. ref.: Tesori 1982, p. 105

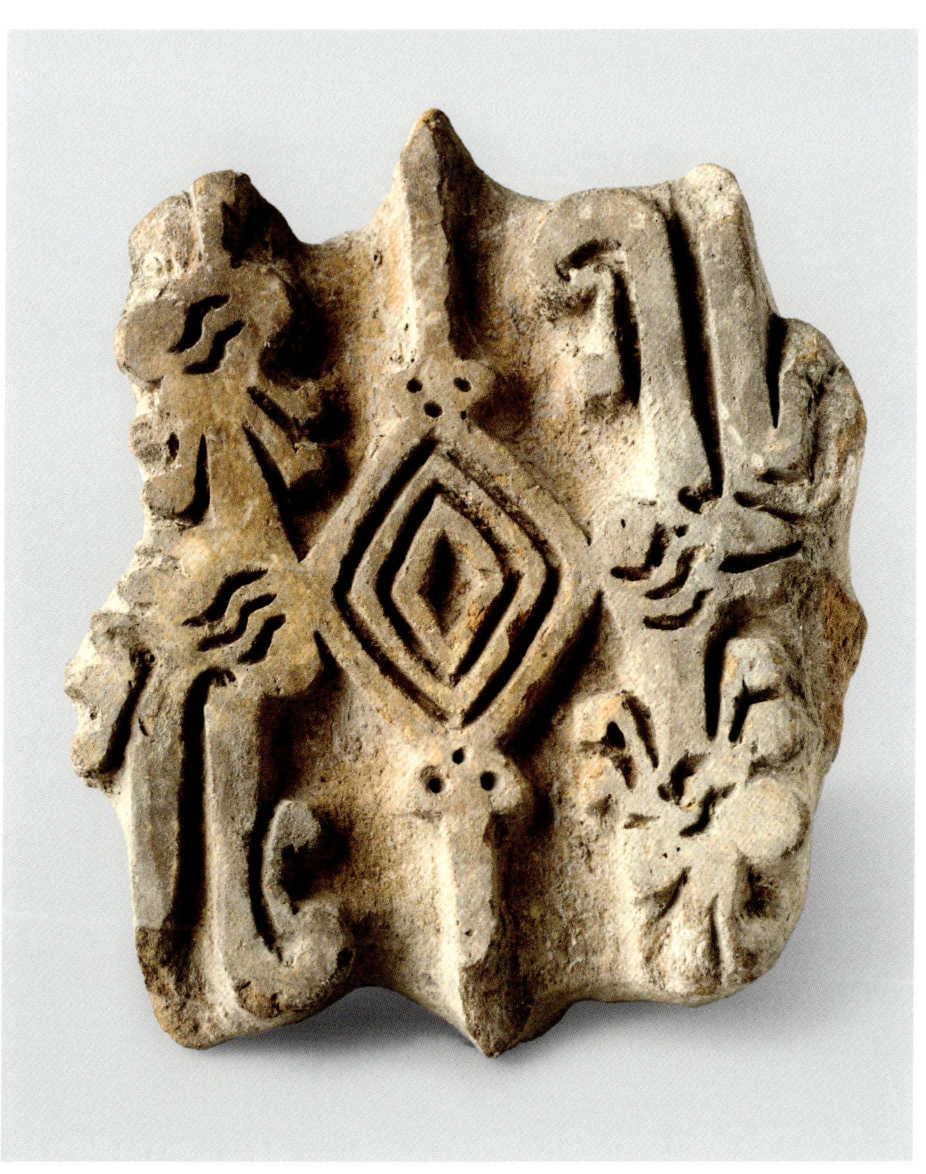

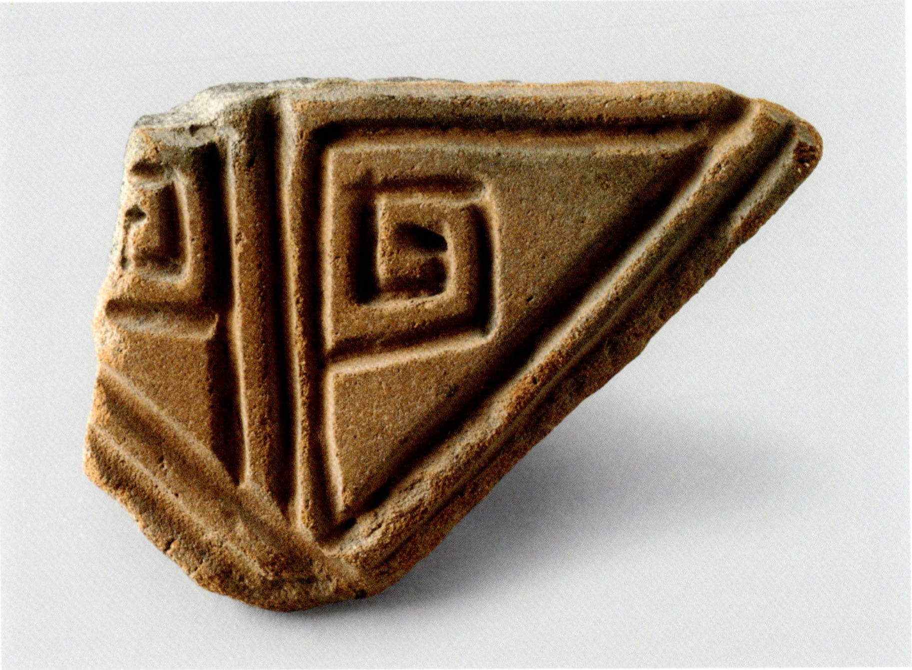

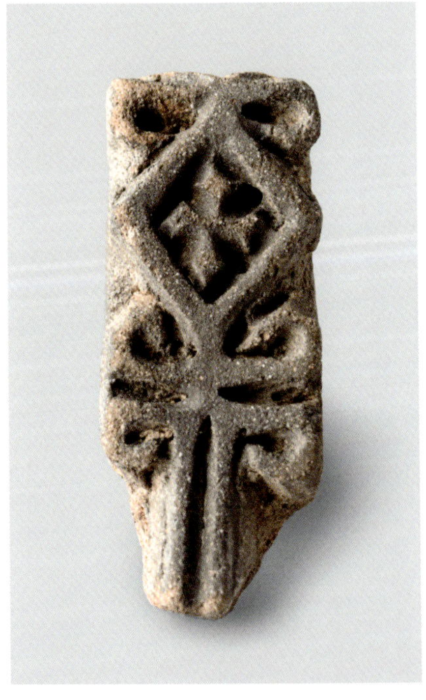

P 27

Culture: uncertain

Dimensions: 39 × 55 × 28

TLT: not available

Object description: flat reddish terracotta with cone-shaped handle at the back

Iconography: stylised face

Condition: fragment lacking the upper left portion. Handle is glued

P 28

Culture: Manteña

Dimensions: 30 × 10 × 30

TLT: not available

Object description: flat brownish terracotta with cone-shaped handle at the back

Iconography: central rhombus is placed horizontally surrounding a cross Along the major diagonal at both ends vertical curls extend symmetrically upward and downward

Condition: the upper part is incomplete

Bibl. ref.: Saville 1907, plate LXXVIII, P 9

Prov.: Gerhard Hirsch Estate, Munich (D), Auction 257, 23–24 September 2008

P 29

Culture: Jama-Coaque

Dimensions: 66 × 22 × 29

TLT: not available

Object description: flat greyish terracotta with cone-shaped handle at the back. Slight convexity

Iconography: inside a quadrangular border stylised twinned figures are placed frontally above stylised patterns that might represent birds

Condition: intact

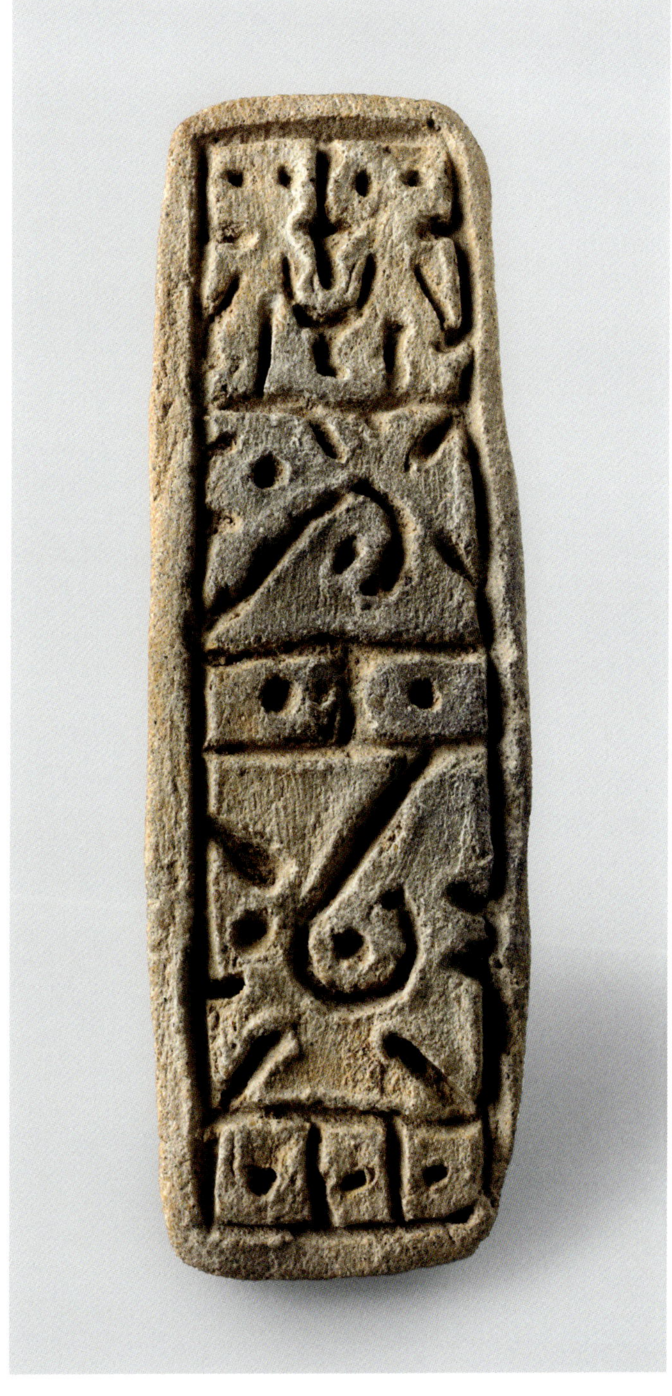

Culture: Jama-Coaque

Dimensions: 70 × 17 × 34

TLT: not available

Object description: flat brownish terracotta with cone-shaped handle at the back

Iconography: abstract pattern placed at the centre of a toothed frame (alternatively one might perceive a mirrored zoomorphic pattern). Twinned figures are placed frontally above and below

Condition: small elements are missing

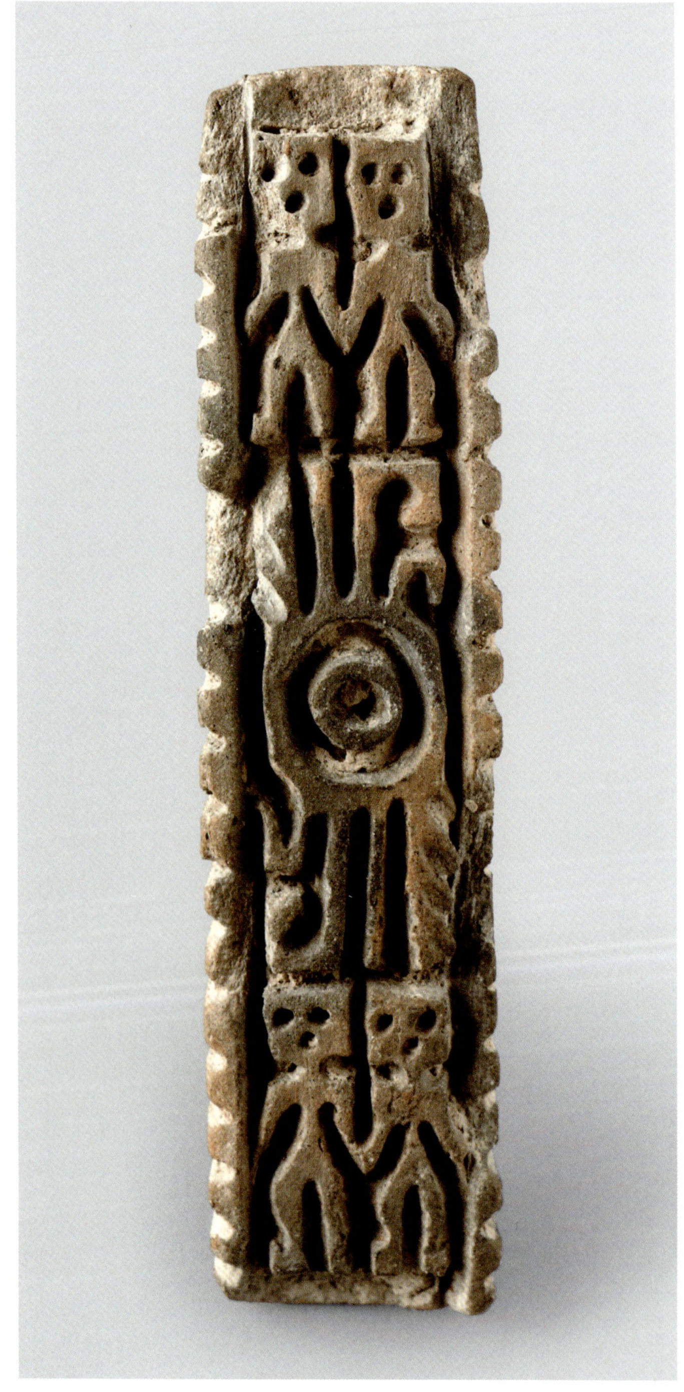

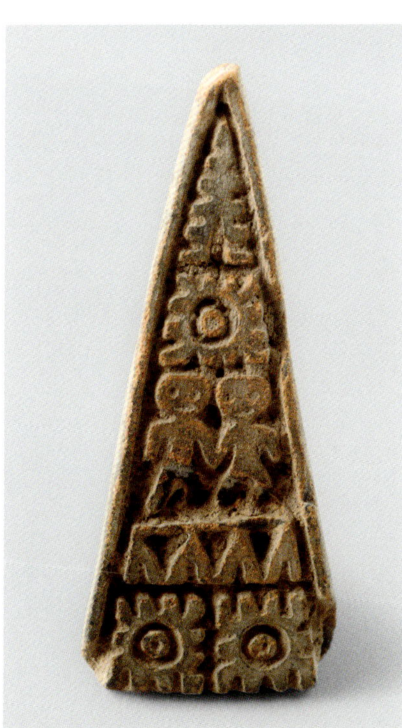

P 31

Culture: Jama-Coaque

Dimensions: 49 × 21 × 33

TLT: not available

Object description: brown-reddish terracotta with cone-shaped handle at the back

Iconography: inside a triangular band two stylised twinned figures are shown frontally holding hands amidst patterns of radiating suns

Condition: intact. Figure shows signs of wear

Prov.: La Canoa / Manabì

P 32

Culture: uncertain

Dimensions: 37 × 60 × 3.6

TLT: not available

Object description: flat grey terracotta with cone-shaped handle at the back

Iconography: twinned stylised and frontal figures are shown in 'praying' position and with turned out legs. Patterns of radiating suns on the chest

Condition: the left portion is missing

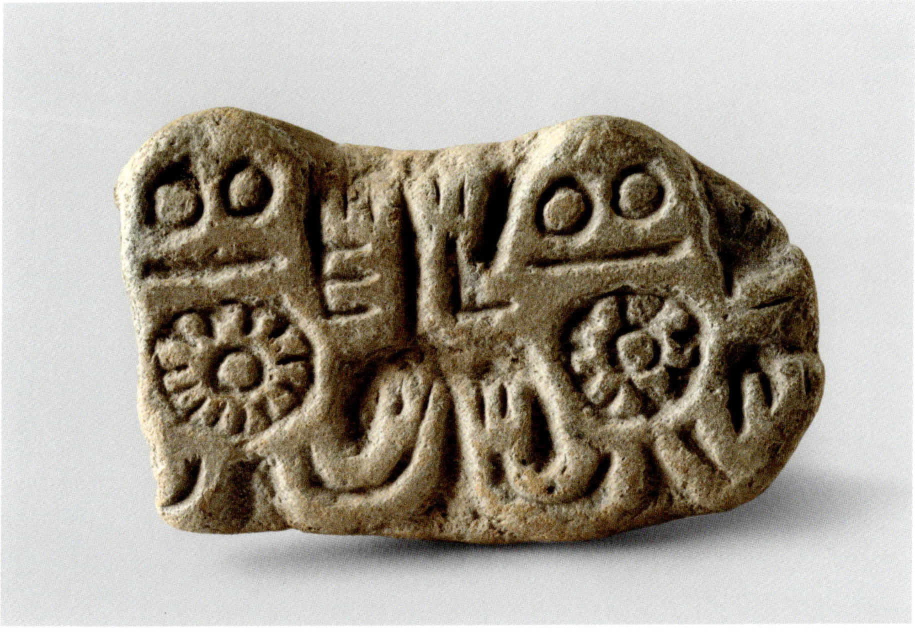

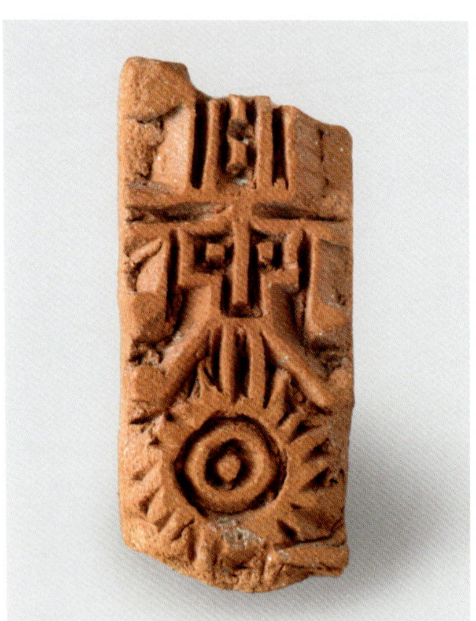

P 33

Culture: uncertain

Dimensions: 29 × 13 × 22

TLT: not available

Object description: flat reddish terracotta with cone-shaped handle at the back

Iconography: Stylised frontal figure with solar emblem in navel (see P 39)

Condition: fragment

P 34

Culture: Manteña

Dimensions: 57 × 67 × 57

TLT: not available

Object description: flat grey terracotta with cone-shaped handle at the back. Slight convexity

Iconography: stylised frontal face

Condition: intact

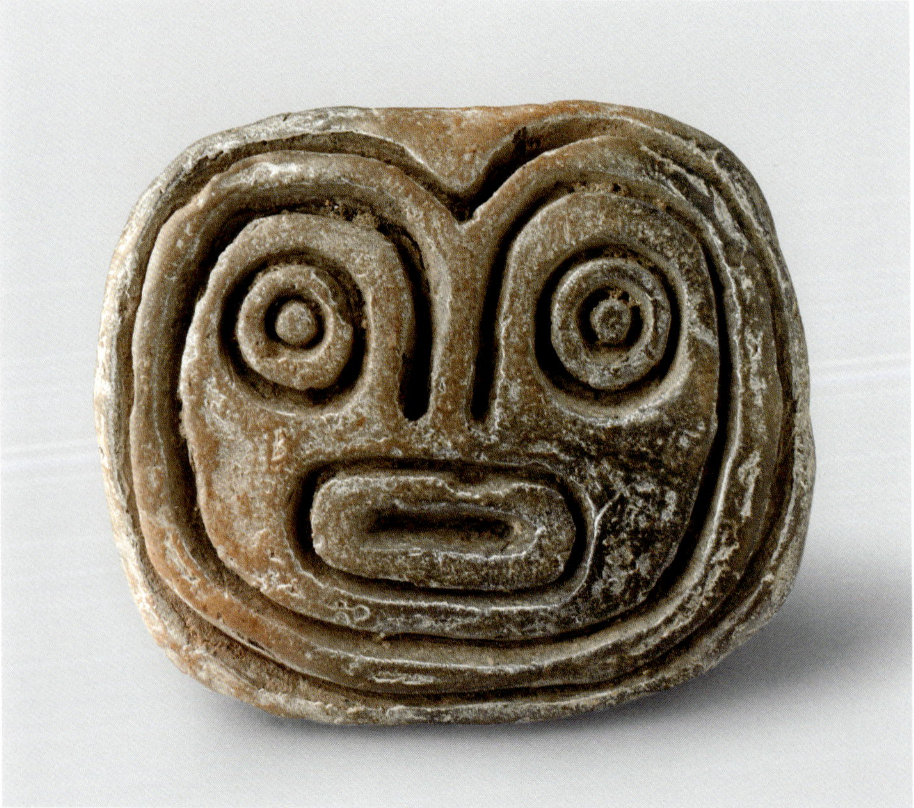

Culture: uncertain

Dimensions: 77 × 41 × 34

TLT: not available

Object description: flat brown-reddish terracotta with cone-shaped handle at the back

Iconography: two vertical tiers inside frame showing toothed indentations at top and bottom. A vertical double band in the middle separates the tiers; each shows stylised faces alternating with radiating (floral?) patterns

Condition: intact

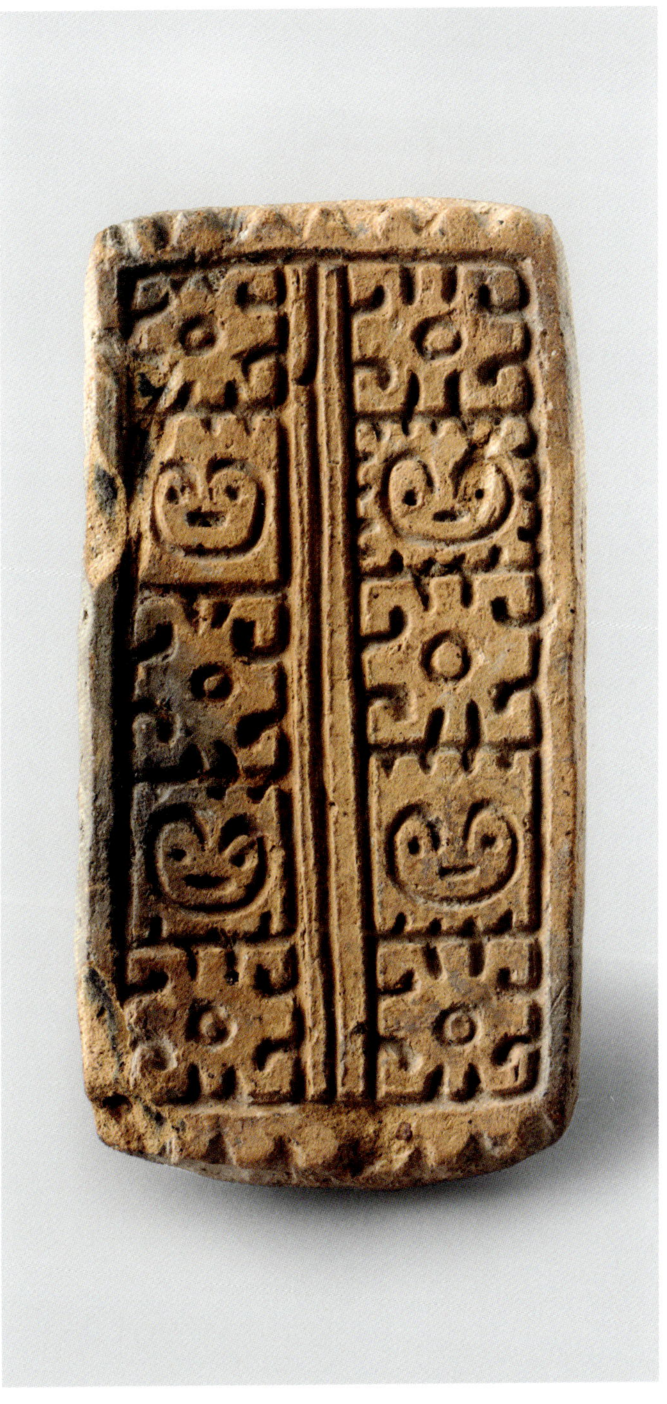

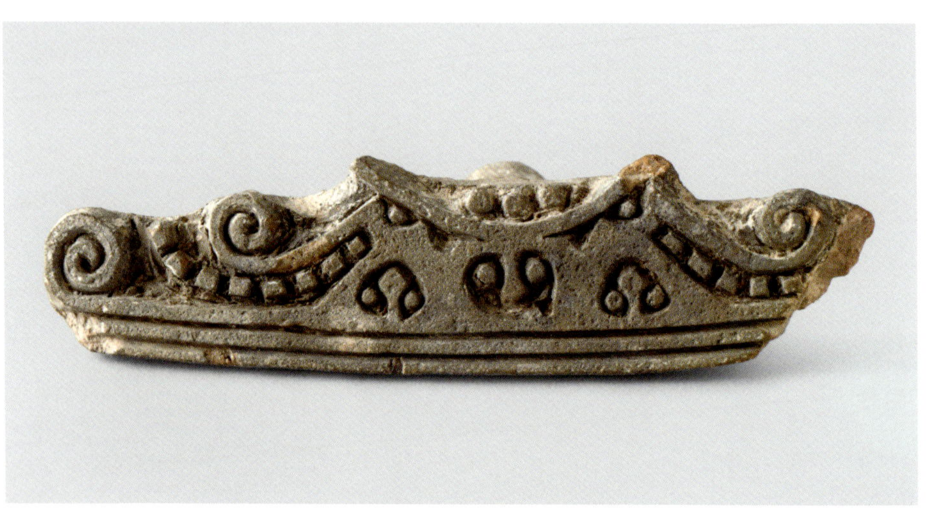

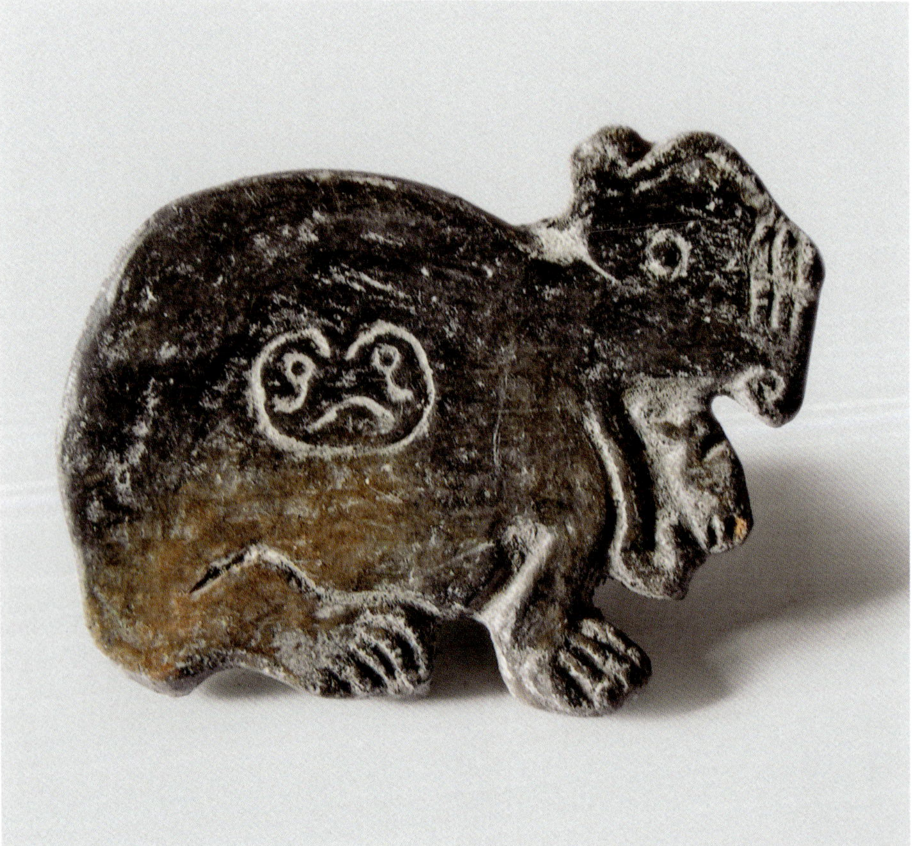

P 36 (left)

Culture: uncertain

Dimensions: 17.5 × 67 × 27.5

TLT: not available

Object description: flat grey terracotta with cone-shaped handle at the back

Iconography: three stylised anthropomorphic faces; the opposite and outer ones are inverted with respect to the central one. The faces are placed within a flat surface that is bound by dotted waved patterns spiralling at the ends. Double band at the bottom

Condition: the right side is incomplete

P 37 (left)

Culture: Manteña

Dimensions: 54 × 71 × 40

TLT: not available

Object description: grey-blackish terracotta with cone-shaped handle at the back

Iconography: animal figure shown in right-facing profile. A bird-like figure appears under the mouth. The body is marked with angry mask

Condition: intact

Prov.: Gerhard Hirsch Estate, Munich (D), Auction 257, 23–24 September 2008

P 38

Culture: uncertain

Dimensions: 22.5 × 25 × 10

TLT: not available

Object description: flat brownish terracotta with cone-shaped handle at the back

Iconography: stylised face possibly showing at the same time the profile of two zoomorphic heads

Condition: fragment with lateral gaps; the handle at the back is partly missing

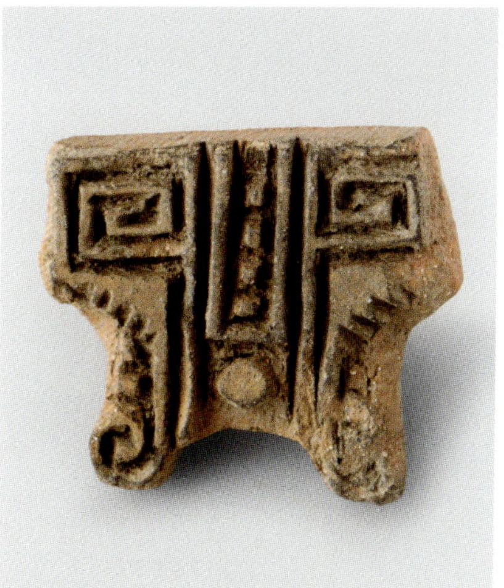

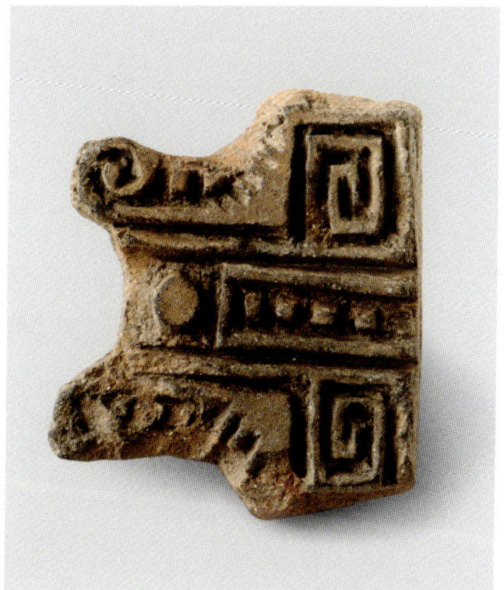

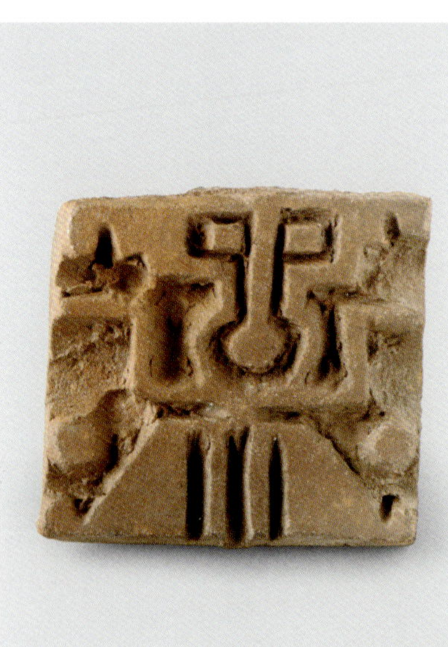

P 39

Culture: uncertain

Dimensions: 33 × 36 × 10

TLT: not available

Object description: flat greyish terracotta

Iconography: stylised frontal figure with arms in 'praying' position (see P 33)

Condition: corner fragment lacking the cone-shaped handle at the back

Prov.: Gerhard Hirsch Estate, Munich (D), Auction 257, 23–24 September 2008

P 40

Culture: Late Jama-Coaque

Dimensions: 58 × 83 × 46

TLT: - 1100 years

Object description: flat grey terracotta with cone-shaped handle at the back

Iconography: stylised frontal mask showing simultaneously two zoomorphic figures profiled looking outward as they stand back to back. Placing by stamping next to each other two images of this *sello*, an image emerges hidden under the form of a second mask, which recalls a jaguar (see also page 19)

Condition: intact

Bibl. ref.: Bodenhorst 1984, p. 43, P 20

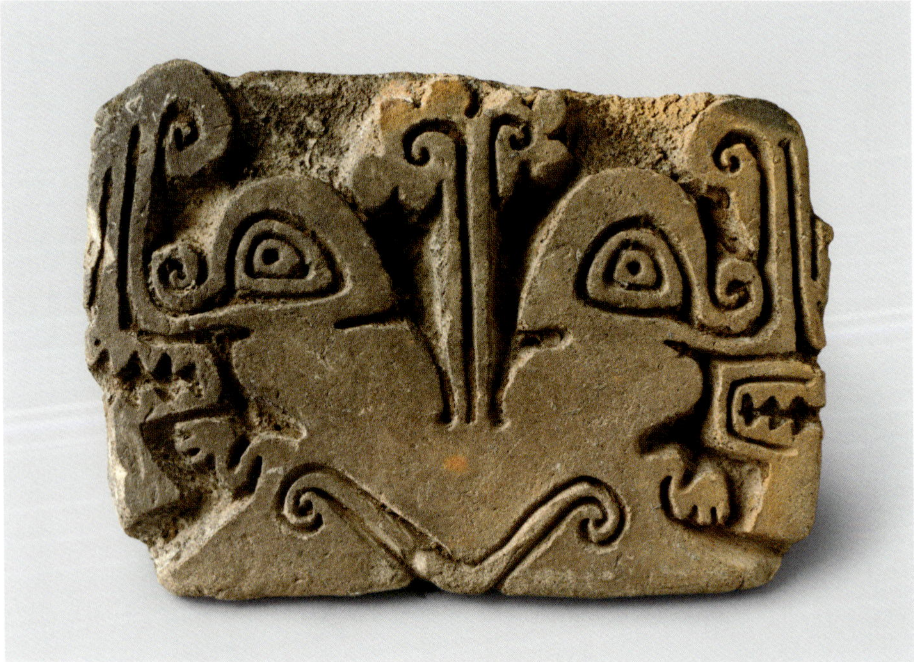

P 41

Culture: Manteña

Dimensions: 58 × 85 × 34

TLT: not available

Object description: flat greyish terracotta with cone-shaped handle at the back

Iconography: stylised frontal face between spirals spreading out (two zoomorphic heads?)

Condition: intact

Prov.: Gerhard Hirsch Estate, Munich (D), Auction 252, 25 September 2007

P 42

Culture: uncertain

Dimensions: 24.5 × 20 × 18.5

TLT: not available

Object description: flat light-coloured terracotta with cone-shaped handle at the back

Iconography: frontal mask?

Condition: small element is missing

Prov.: Gerhard Hirsch Estate, Munich (D), Auction 257, 23–24 September 2008

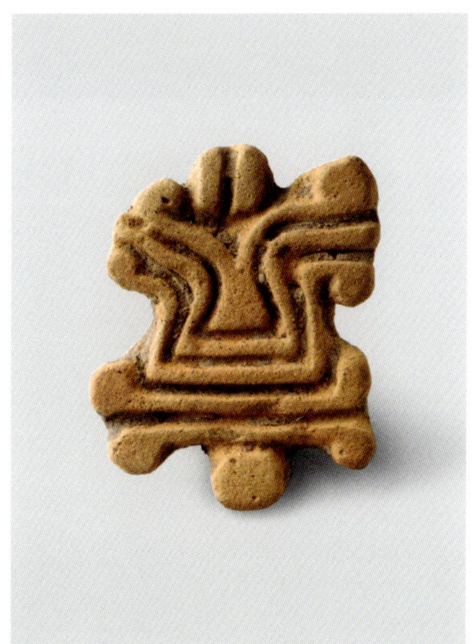

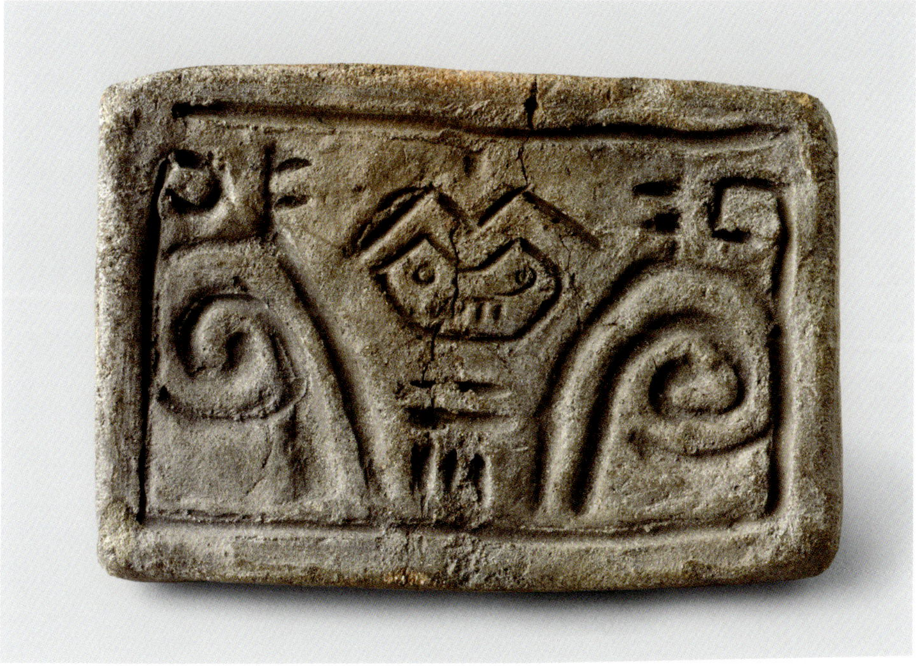

P 43

Culture: La Tolita

Dimensions: 49 × 83 × 48

TLT: not available

Object description: flat grey terracotta with cone-shaped handle at the back

Iconography: stylised frontal mask showing simultaneously the profile of two zoomorphic figures (jaguars) looking outward as they stand back to back

Condition: glued in parts

Ref.: Museo 1966, fig, 11

P 44 (right)

Culture: Coast of Esmeraldas (late Jama-Coaque)

Dimensions: 65 × 48 × 35

TLT: not available

Object description: flat brownish terracotta with cone-shaped handle at the back

Iconography: stylised left hand with anti-clockwise spiral on the palm

Condition: incomplete

Bibl. ref.: Anton 1974, p. 11; Estrada 1959, no. 78

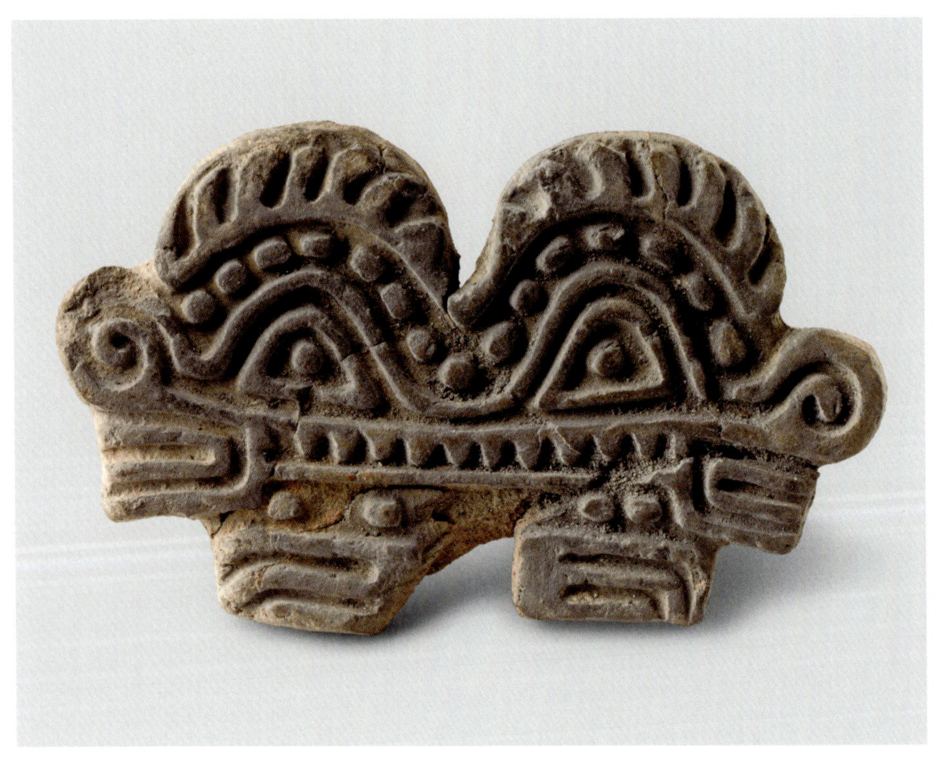

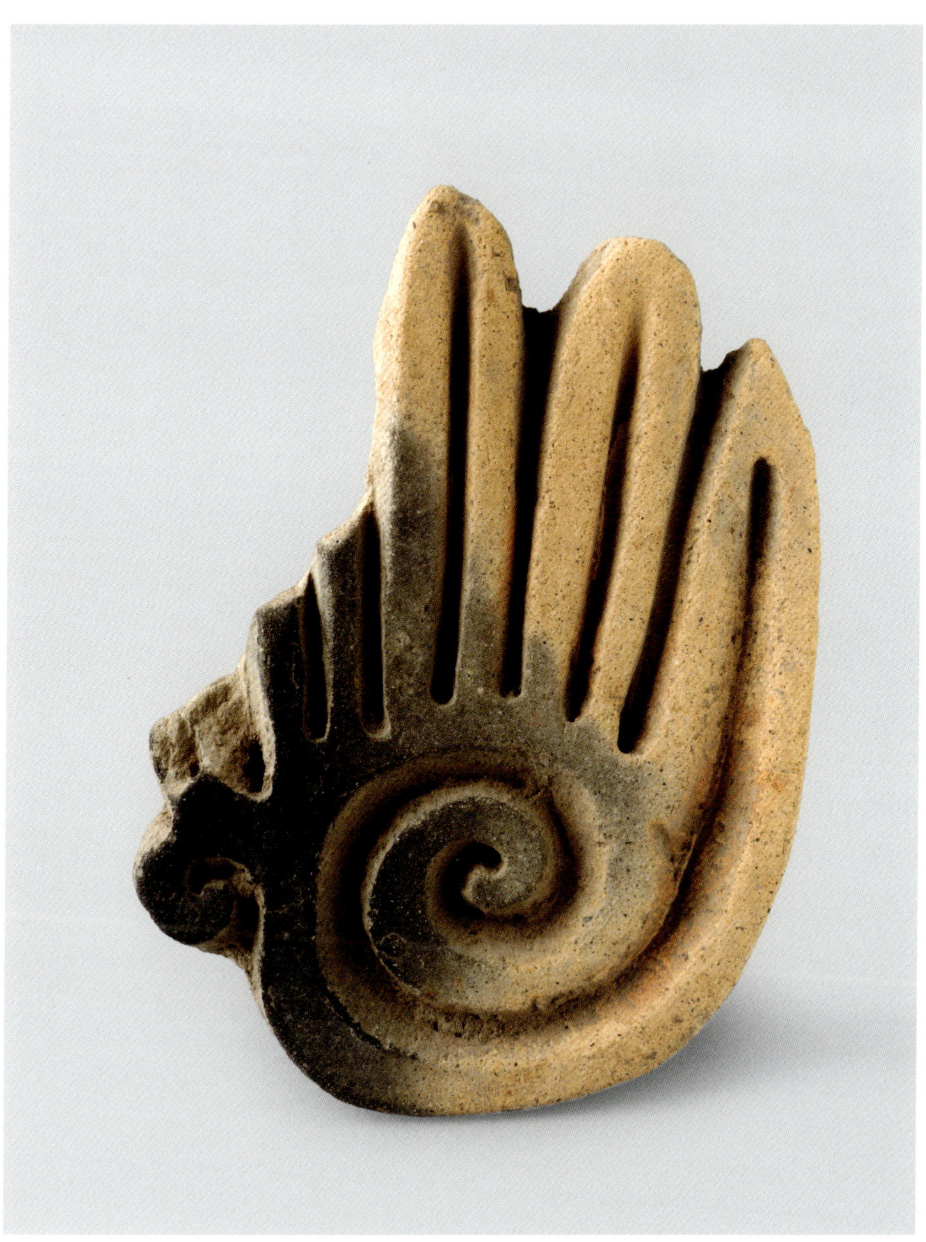

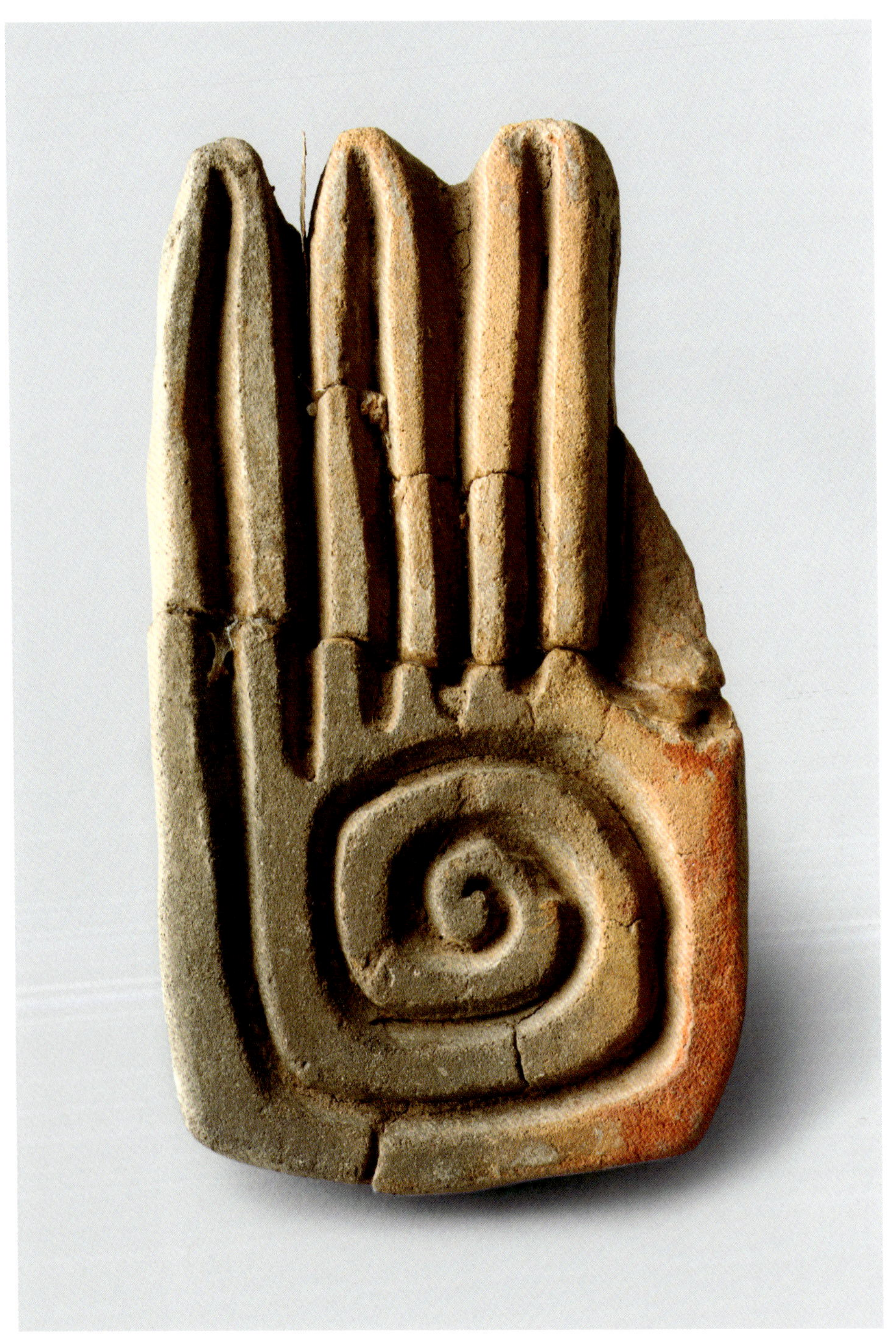

P 45 (left)

Culture: Coast of Esmeraldas (late Jama-Coaque)

Dimensions: 105 × 59 × 65

TLT: - 750 years

Object description: flat brownish terracotta with cone-shaped handle at the back. Traces of red colouring

Iconography: stylised right hand with clockwise spiral on the palm

Condition: incomplete and glued

Bibl. ref.: Anton 1974, p. 11; Estrada 1959, no. 78

P 46

Culture: Coast of Esmeraldas (late Jama-Coaque)

Dimensions: 37 × 50 × 45

TLT: not available

Object description: flat brownish terracotta with cone-shaped handle at the back

Iconography: stylised hand with clockwise spiral on the palm

Condition: the upper part is missing

Bibl. ref.: Cummins & Burgos 1996, p. 155 fig. 68 a, b, c

P 47

Culture: uncertain

Dimensions: 22.5 × 28 × 12

TLT: not available

Object description: flat greyish terracotta with cone-shaped handle at the back

Iconography: pair of stylised symmetrically placed hands and double S pattern on the palm. Two spirals on the palm are both curled in the same direction. When rotating counterclockwise one might see simultaneously the profiles of two zoomorphic faces looking to the right

Condition: the handle at the back is missing

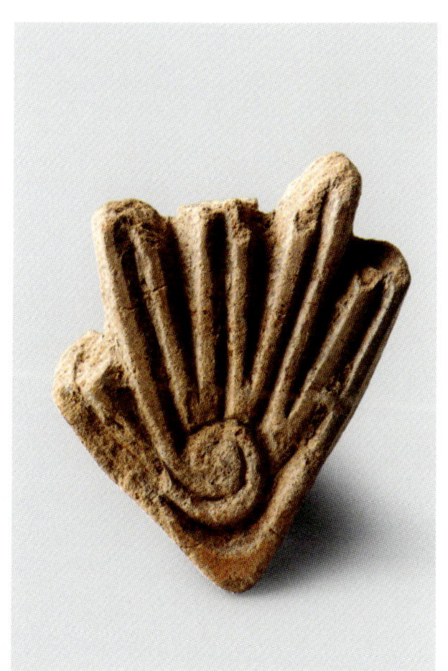

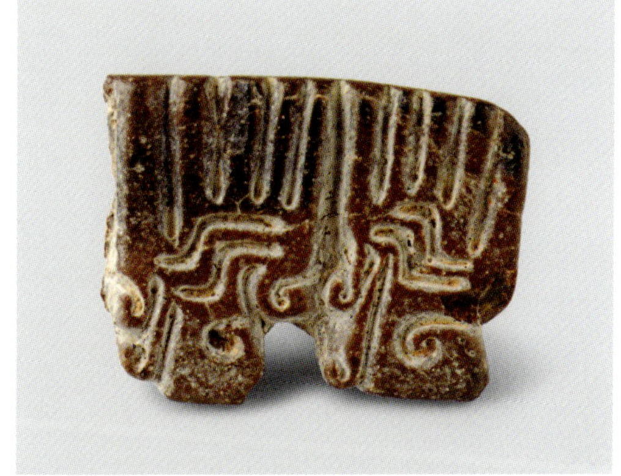

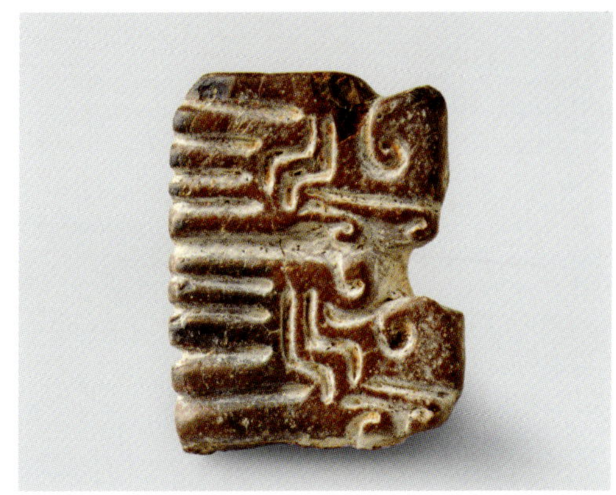

P 48

Culture: Manteña

Dimensions: 116 × 27 × 30

TLT: not available

Object description: flat brownish terracotta with greyish shadings with cone-shaped handle at the back

Iconography: in the middle masked and tailed figure with head shown in profile facing left and body frontally positioned, possibly wearing a belt. The right hand is extended and the left one is bent and holds in the hand a moon-shaped blade (?). Above and underneath are two rhombuses placed horizontally along the major axis. The upper and lower corners develop into two outward curling symmetric spirals

Condition: badly damaged diagonal fracture that has been glued

Prov.: Gerhard Hirsch Estate, Munich (D), Auction 252, 25 September 2007

P 49

Culture: Coast of Manabì (late Jama-Coaque)

Dimensions: 10 × 21 × 25

TLT: - 1150 years

Object description: flat brown terracotta with greyish shadings, with cylindrical handle at the back

Iconography: very small *sello* showing in the centre a solar pattern between two trident-shaped images with three-pointed heads

Condition: worn

Bibl. ref.: Saville 1907, plate LXXVIII, fig. 7

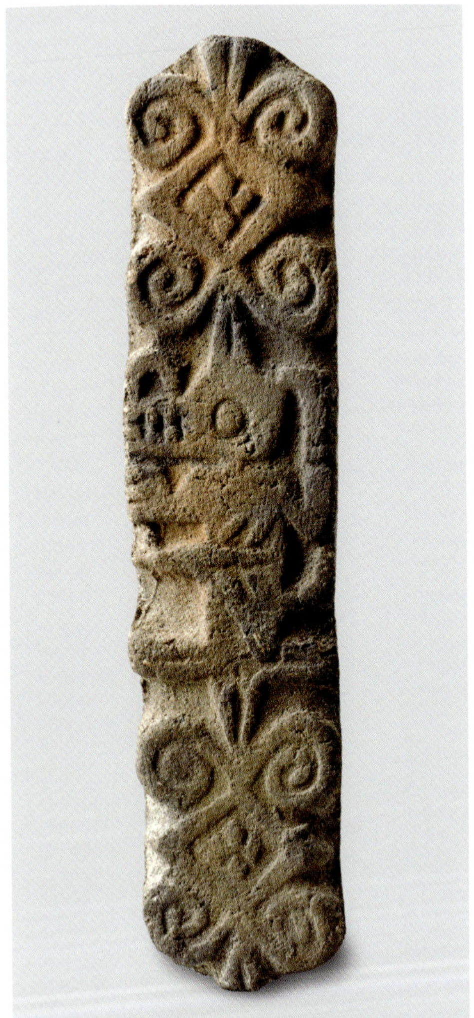

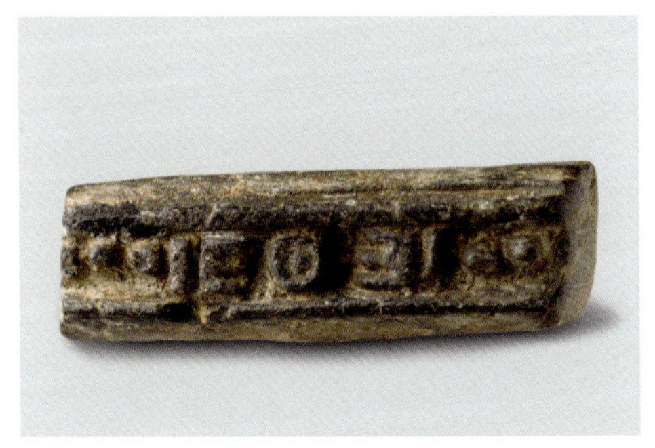

P 50

Culture: uncertain

Dimensions: 53 × 55 × 48

TLT: not available

Object description: flat brownish terracotta with cone-shaped handle at the back

Iconography: free shapes placed between two circular bands joined below. Masks? The top of the handle may represent a worn out zoomorphic point

Condition: the inferior socket is missing

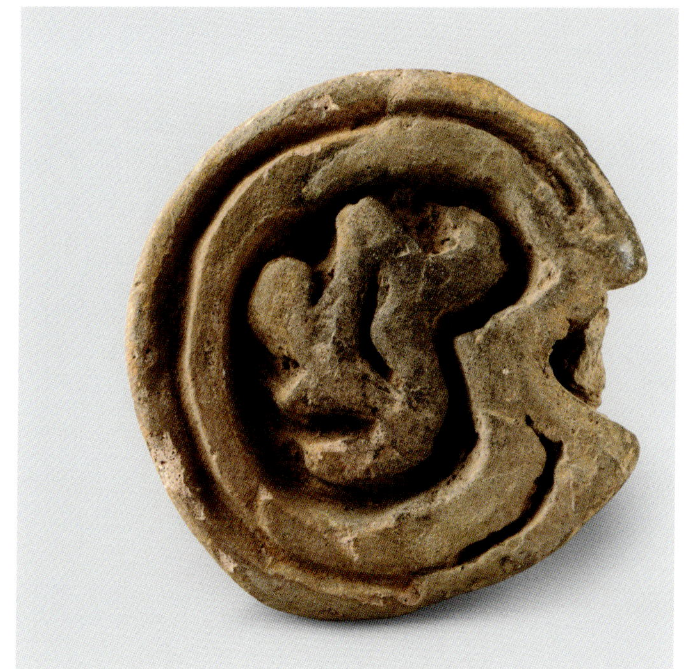

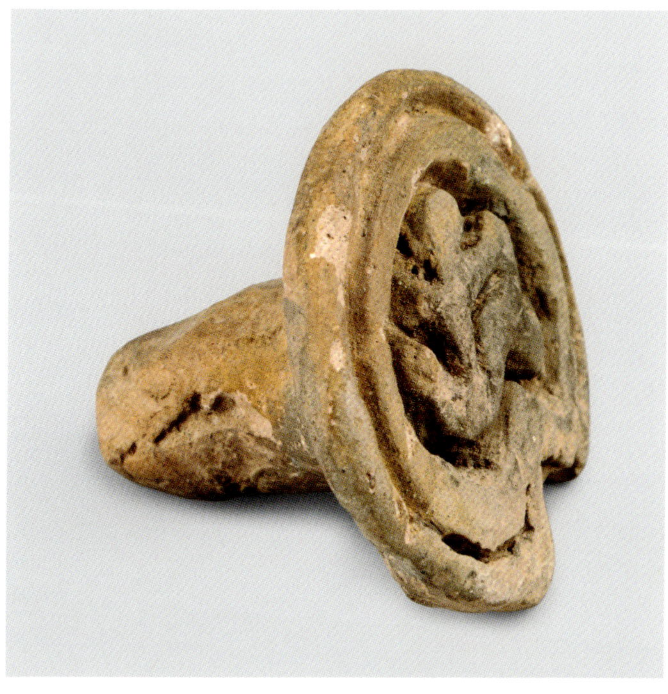

P 51

Culture: Manteña

Dimensions: 21 × 36 × 26

TLT: not available

Object description: flat reddish terracotta with cone-shaped handle at the back

Iconography: two zoomorphic figures facing each other

Note: a peculiarity of this *sello* is that it might be read both as positive and negative. Impressing the *sello* as positive, an image emerges hidden under the form of a mask, which resembles a jaguar

Condition: the top right corner is missing

Bibl. ref.: Parducci 1966: Lamina no. 4., fig. b

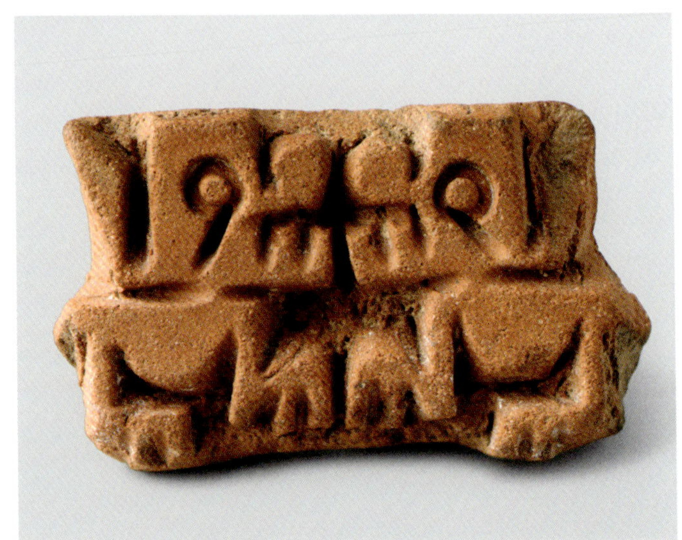

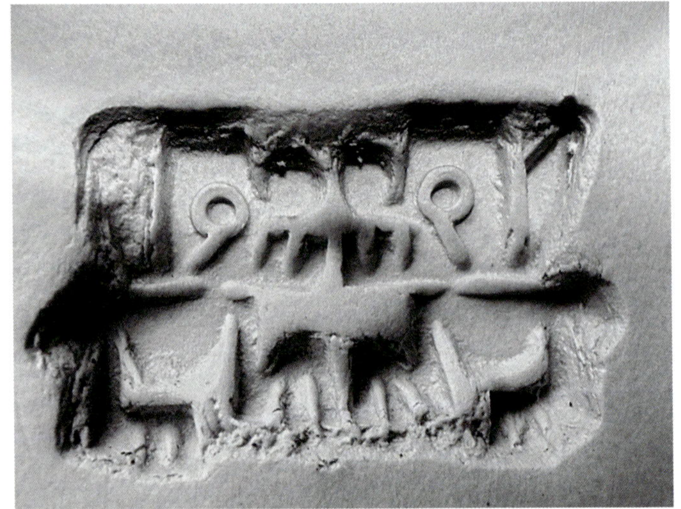

Culture: uncertain

Dimensions: 15 × 38 × 22.5

TLT: not available

Object description: flat blackish terracotta with cone-shaped handle at the back

Iconography: banded horizontal borders enclose spirals alternating with vertical bands. The top of the handle shows a crossed incision

Condition: lateral segments are missing

Prov: Gerhard Hirsch Estate, Munich (D). Auction 257, 23–24 September 2008

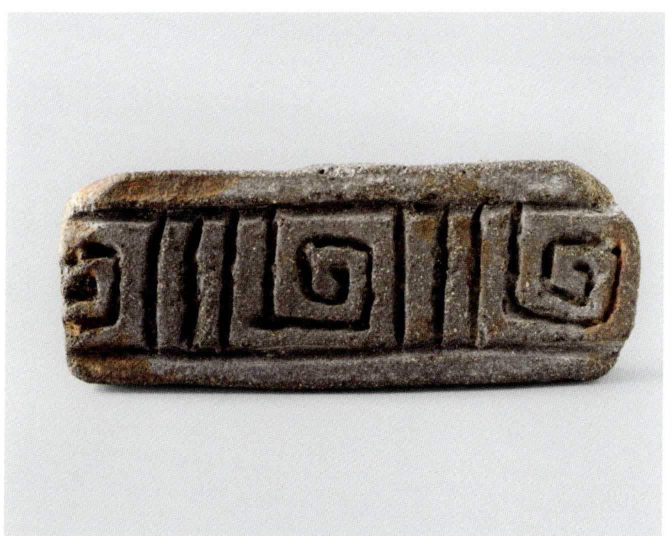

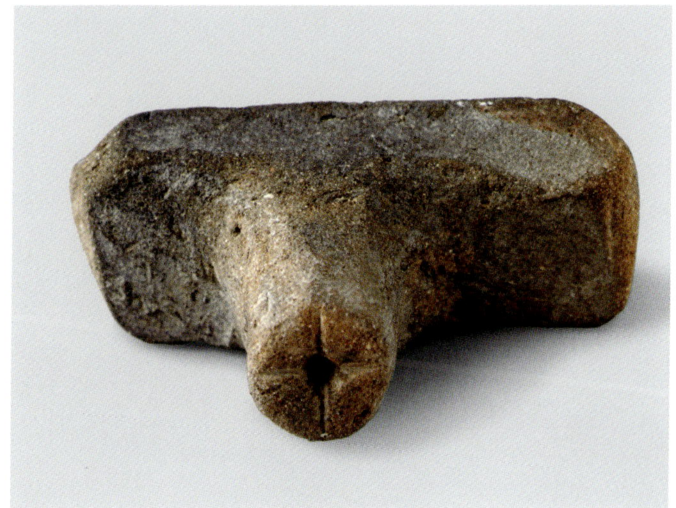

P 53

Culture: uncertain

Dimensions: 68 × 58 × 33

TLT: 700 years

Object description: flat *sello* made of brown-greyish terracotta. Fragment lacking the cone-shaped handle at the back

Iconography: four diagonal arms emanate from a radiating centre. Symbolic representation of the sun and the four corners of the earth and the created world

Condition: half of the *sello* is missing (has been intentionally divided off along the middle)

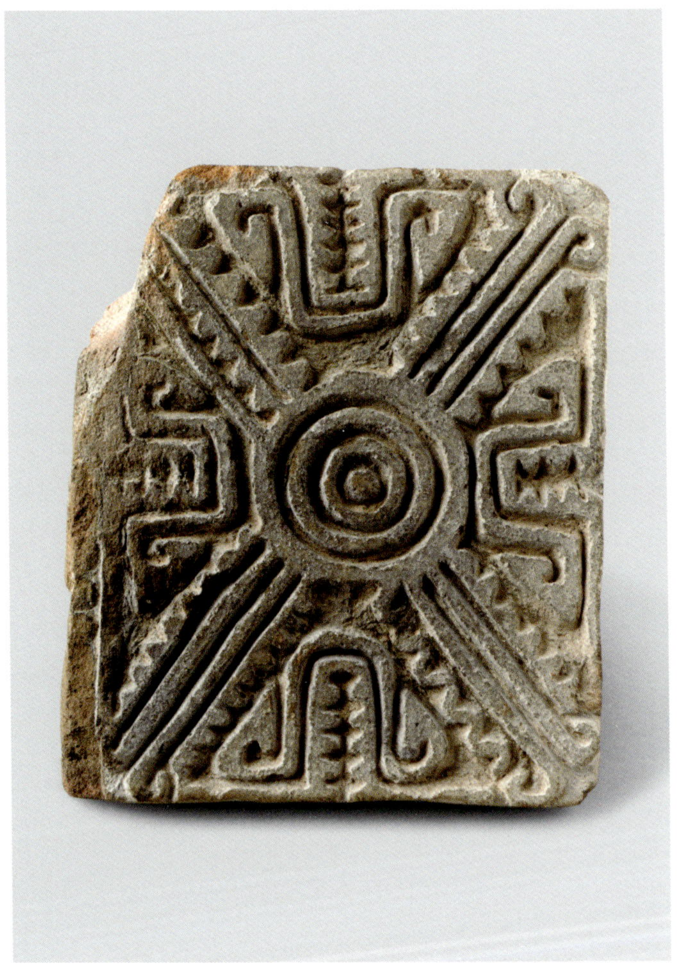

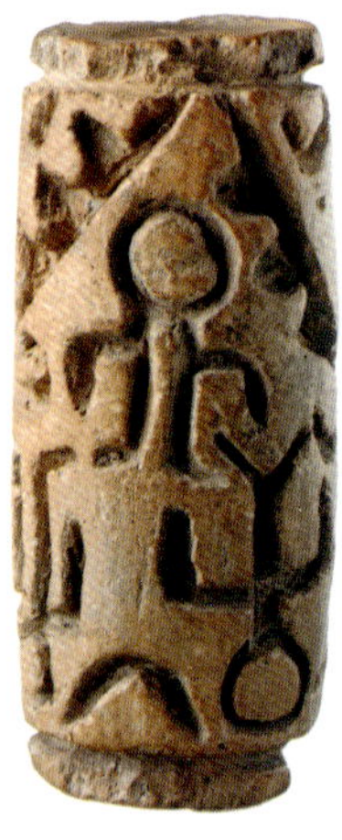

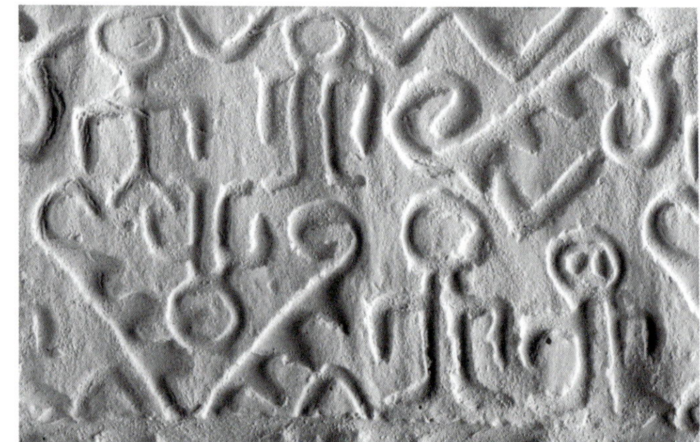

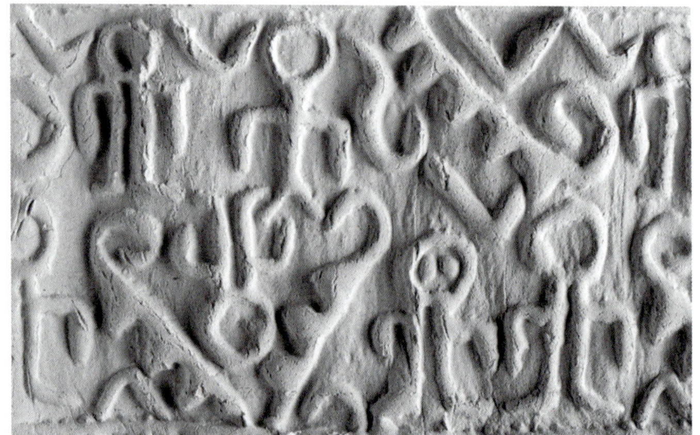

C 1

Culture: Coast of Manabì
(late Jama-Coaque)

Dimensions: 63 × 27

TLT: - 1000 years

Object description:
cylindrical *sello* made of
brownish terracotta, no axial
perforation

Iconography: a number of
anthropomorphic figures
placed between V-shaped
patterns with step-like
excretions and distal curl.
Narrow circular
indentations at both ends

Note: a peculiarity of this
sello is that it might be read
both as positive and negative
(see reproduction)

Condition: the ring-shaped
bands at both ends are
fractured

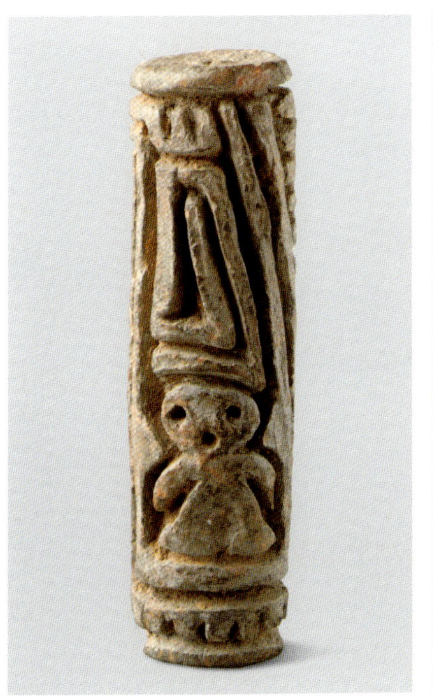 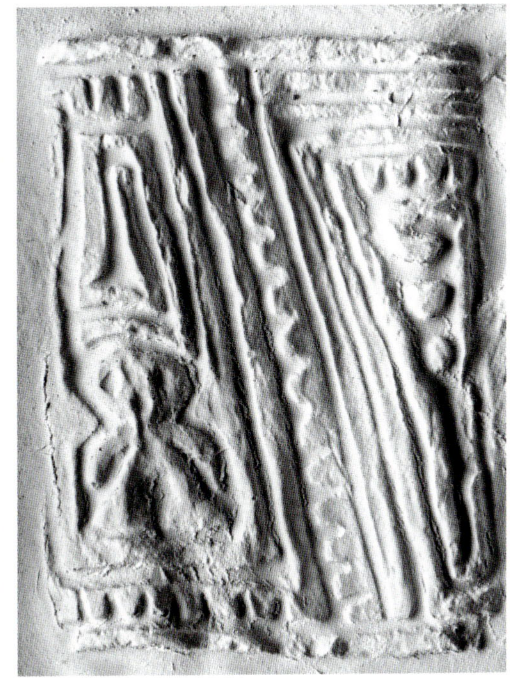

C 2

Culture: Jama-Coaque

Dimensions: 61 × 17

TLT: not available

Object description:
cylindrical *sello* made of
brownish terracotta, axially
perforated Ø 3

Iconography:
anthropomorphic figure
supporting on its head a
triangular spiral topped by
trident-like pattern. The
figure is flanked by a slanted
band followed by a toothed
one, which is detached from
a convoluted abstract theme
with two points at its centre,
surrounded by angled
bands. Narrow circular
indentations at both ends

Condition: intact

C 3

Culture: late Jama-Coaque

Dimensions: 71 × 28

TLT: - 1200 years

Object description:
cylindrical *sello* made of
brownish terracotta, axially
perforated Ø 7

Iconography: two
superimposed tiers, each
showing a pattern of
twinned anthropomorphic
figures holding hands and
associated with toothed
patterns, alternating with
spiral themes with possible
zoomorphic allusions. The
two tiers are offset against
each other, and the spirals
are mirror images.
Underneath the lower tier is
a thin toothed pattern

Condition: the ring-shaped
bands at both ends are
broken off

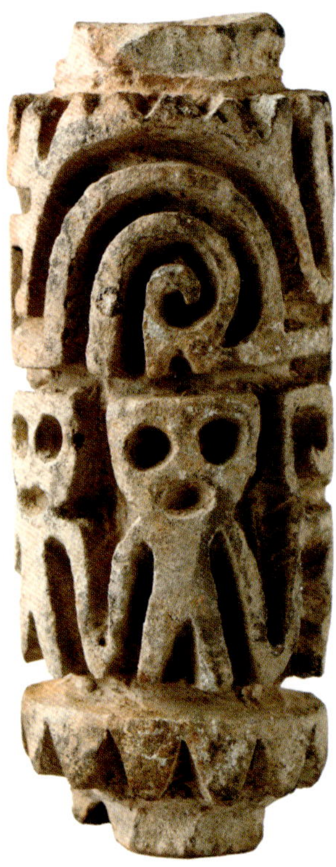

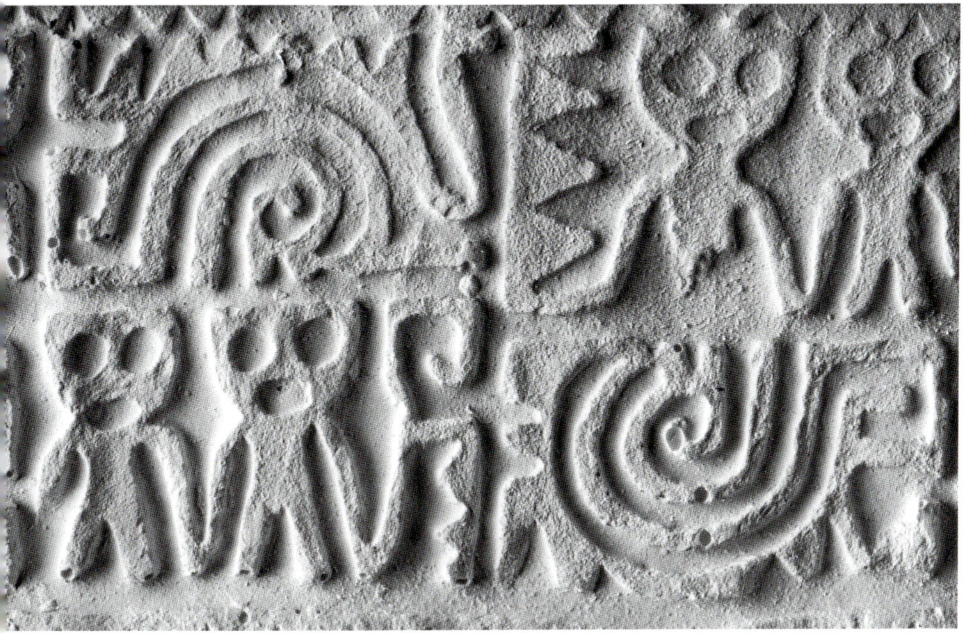

C 4

Culture: Jama-Coaque

Dimensions: 57 × 26

TLT: not available

Object description: cylindrical *sello* made of orange-brownish terracotta, axially perforated Ø 7

Iconography: two superimposed tiers, each showing a pattern of twinned figures inside a square frame (one of them might be associated with a zoomorphic subject) followed by concentric banded triangles separated by knobbed diagonal. The squares are offset and mirrored. Underneath the tiers there is a thin circular indentation

Condition: one terminal annulet is missing

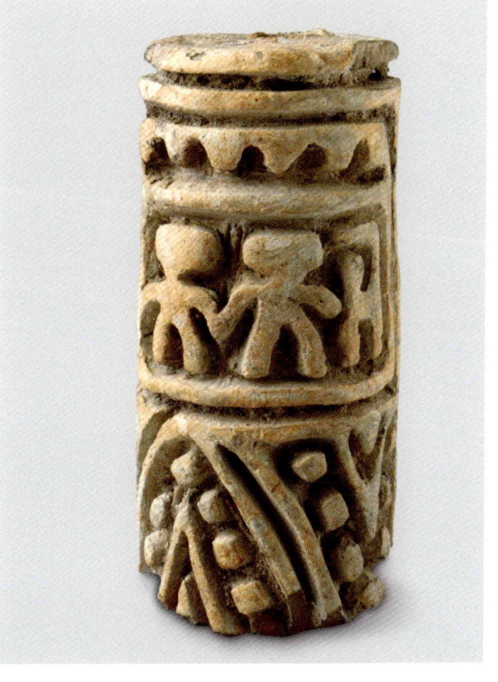

C 5

Culture: Jama-Coaque

Dimensions: 42 × 28

TLT: not available

Object description: fragment of cylindrical *sello* made of brownish terracotta, axially perforated Ø 3

Iconography: row of anthropomorphic figures holding hands placed under a ring-shaped band with toothed lower edge

Condition: the lower tier is missing

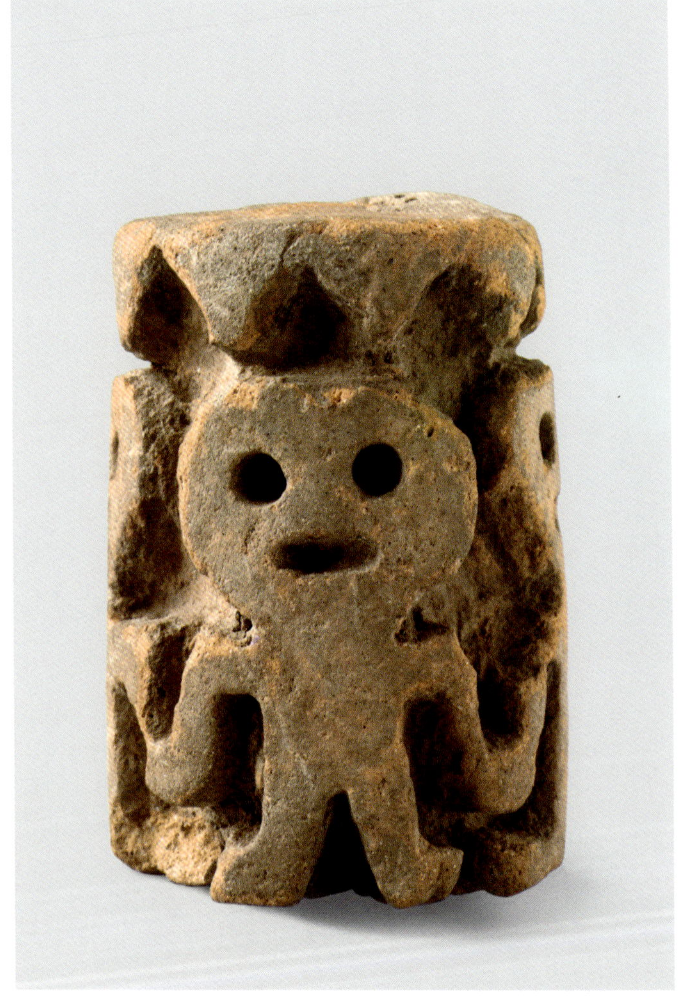

Culture: Jama-Coaque

Dimensions: 37 × 28

TLT: not available

Object description: fragment of cylindrical *sello* made of brownish terracotta, axially perforated Ø 7

Iconography: row of anthropomorphic figures holding hands placed between ring-shaped bands

Condition: the lower tier is missing

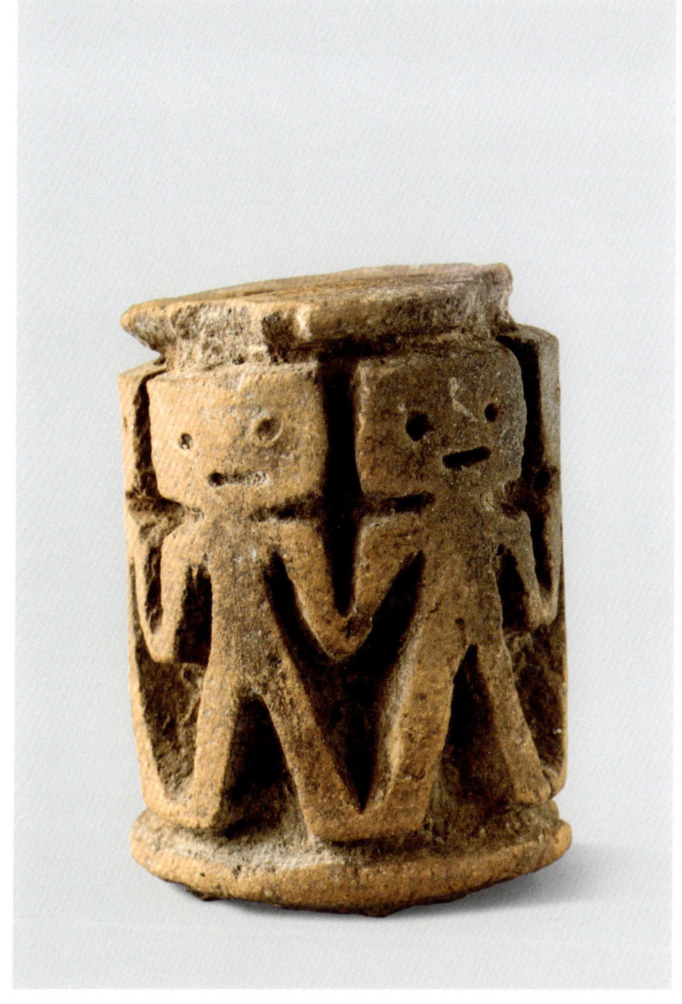

Culture: Jama-Coaque

Dimensions: 54 × 31

TLT: not available

Object description: fragment of cylindrical *sello* made of dark terracotta, axially perforated Ø 12

Iconography: row of anthropomorphic figures holding hands placed between two ring-shaped bands. The upper band above the row consists of a row of dot-shaped knobs and a plain ring. The lower end shows a series of graven points

Condition: the lower tier is missing

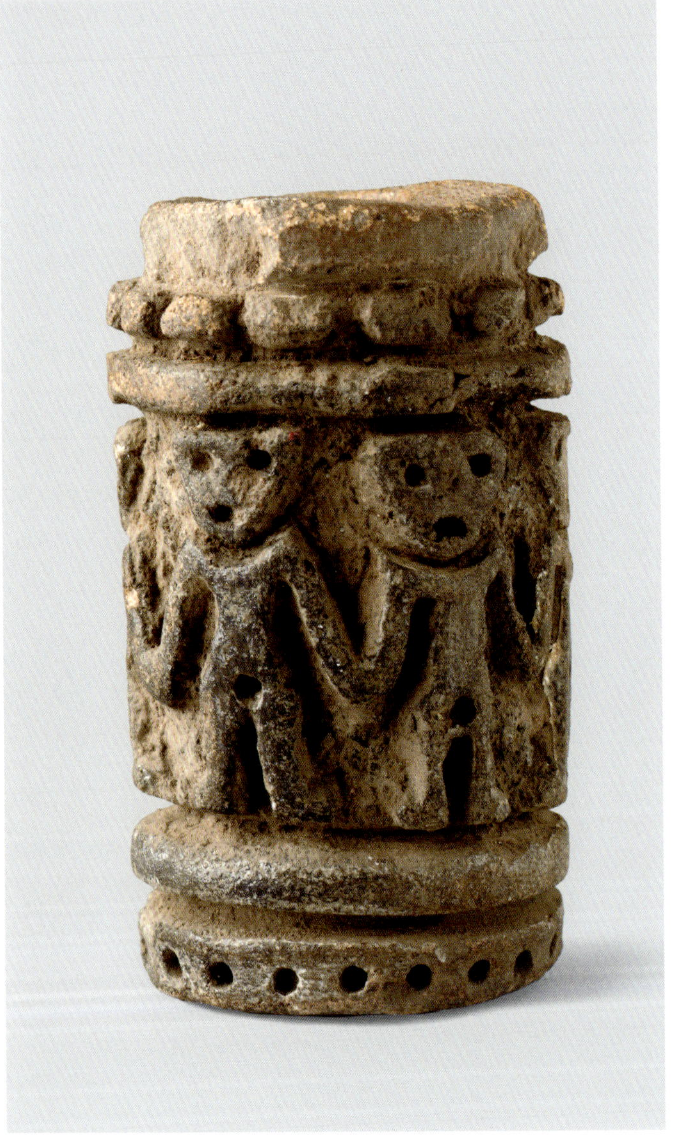

Culture: uncertain

Dimensions: 5.7 × 2.6

TLT: not available

Object description: fragment of cylindrical *sello* made of brownish terracotta, no axial perforation

Iconography: the vertical sequence begins at the top with a series of dot-shaped knobs placed between plain ring-shaped bands, followed underneath by a row of anthropomorphic figures holding hands, and finally a row of four-pointed stars

Condition: the lower tier is broken off and missing

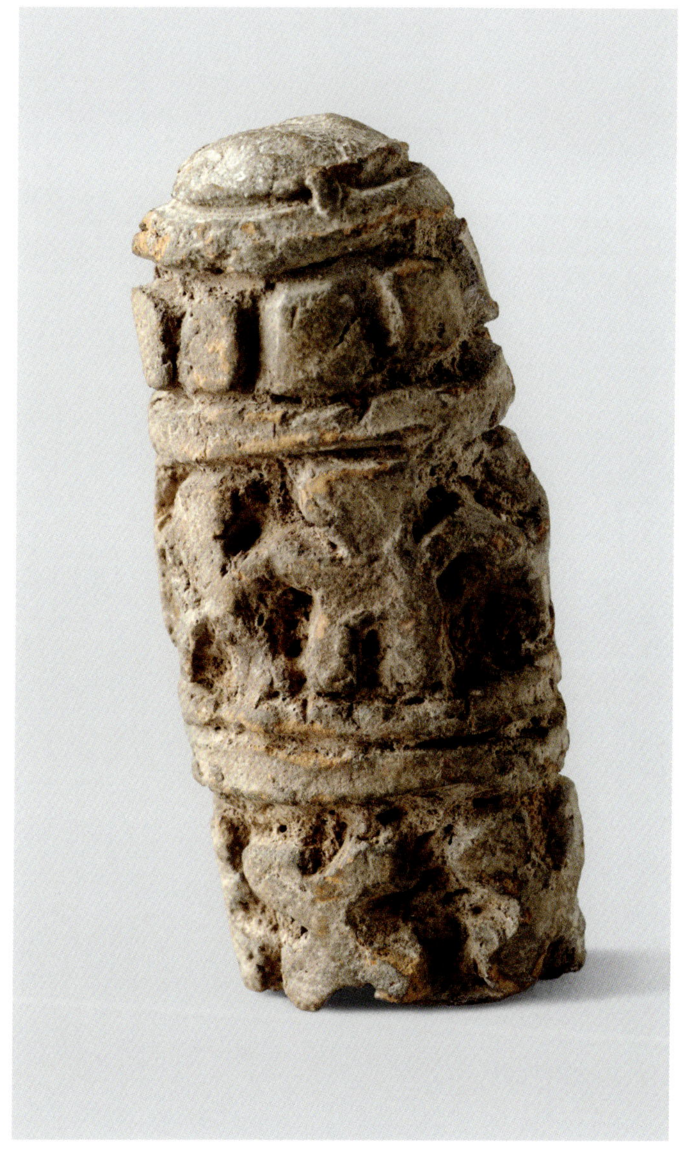

C 9

Culture: Jama-Coaque

Dimensions: 79 × 31

TLT: not available

Object description:
cylindrical *sello* made of
brownish terracotta, axially
perforated Ø 14

Iconography: two
superimposed tiers, each
showing a row of
anthropomorphic figures
holding hands. The rows are
set off against each other. A
middle section, consisting of
a central row of dot-shaped
knobs placed between
toothed bands (the tooth
pointing downward) and
plain ring-shaped bands

Condition: object is broken
into two parts along a
median longitudinal fracture
line and glued. Traces of
abrasions at both ends might
indicate smoothing after
extremities had broken off

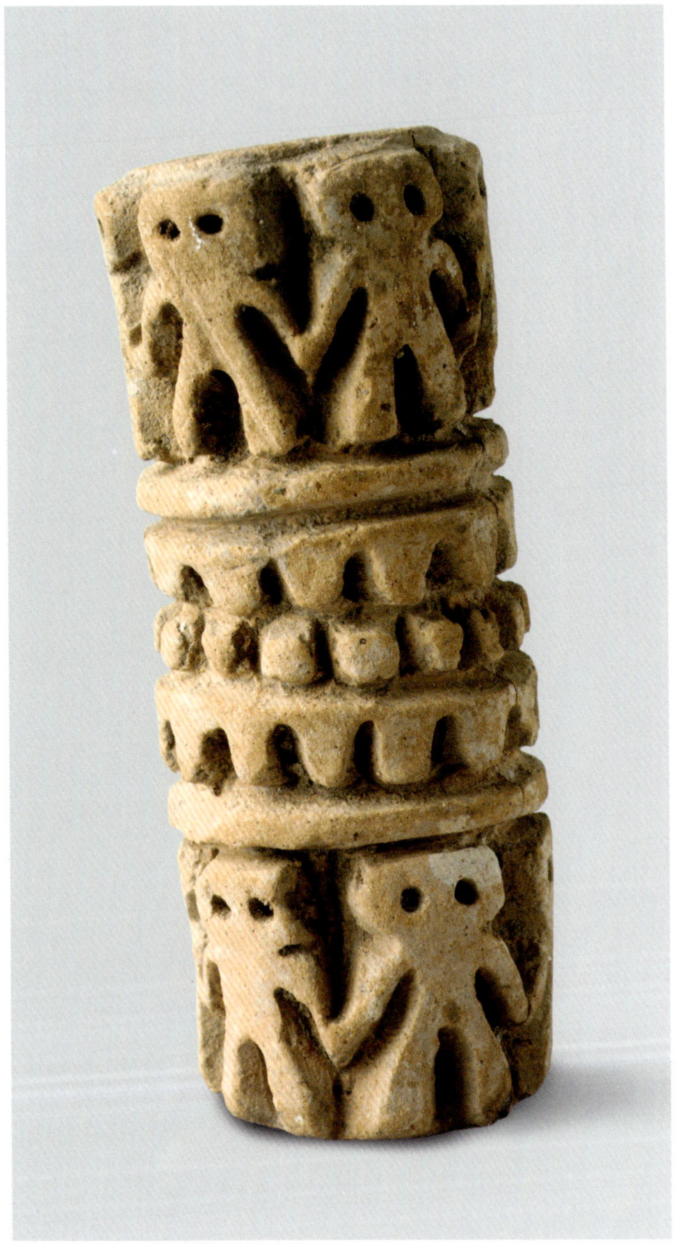

Culture: uncertain

Dimensions: 68 × 29

TLT: not available

Object description: semi-cylindrical *sello* made of dark terracotta, not axially perforated. Back shows no trace of fractures or smoothing. Traces of pink pigmentation on both front and back

Iconography: two superimposed tiers, each showing a row of anthropomorphic figures joined at hands and feet. The two tiers are bounded by ring-shaped bands

Condition: front side intact, back worn out

Prov.: Estate of Gerhard Hirsch, Munich (D), Auction 257, 23–24 September 2008

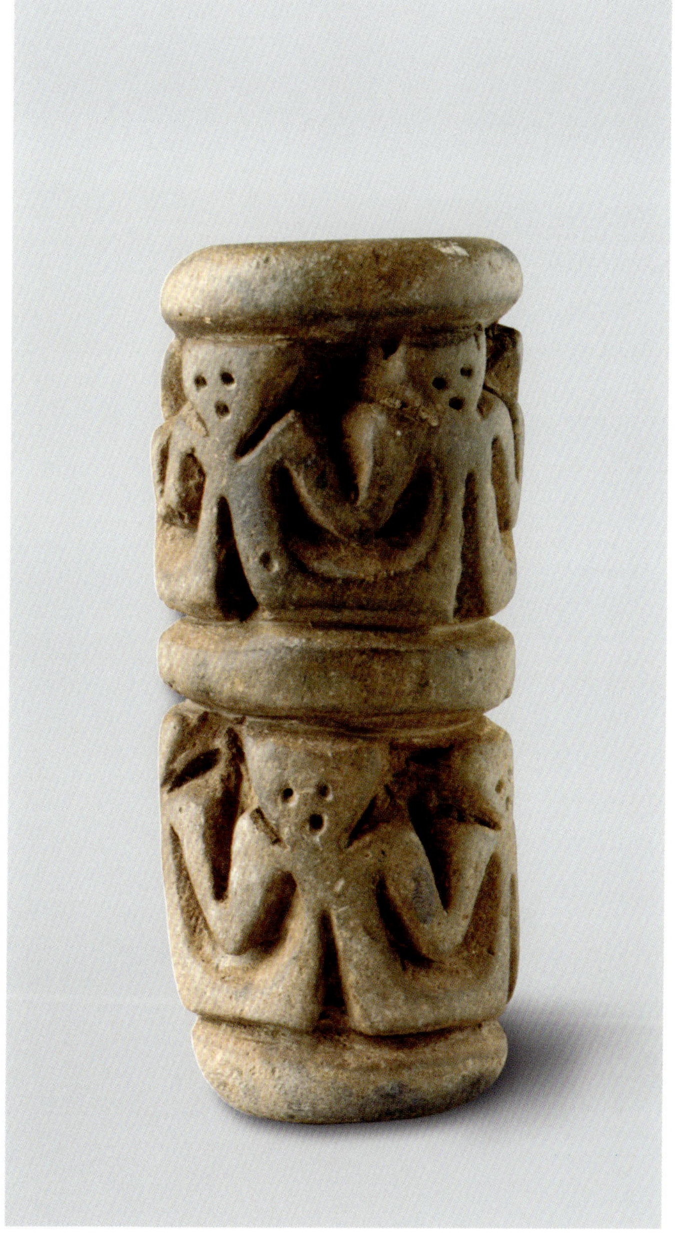

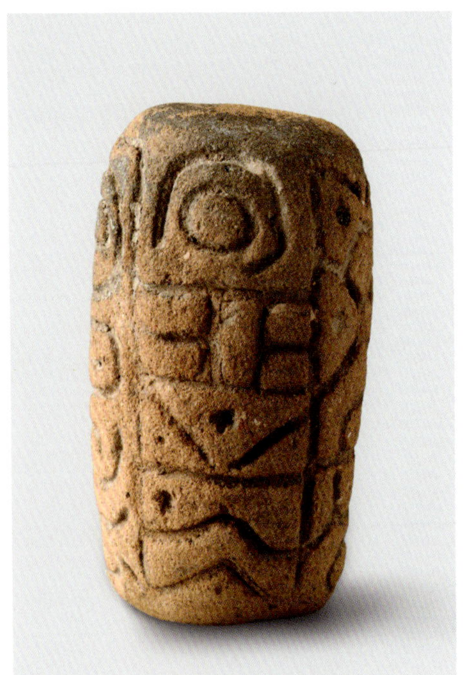 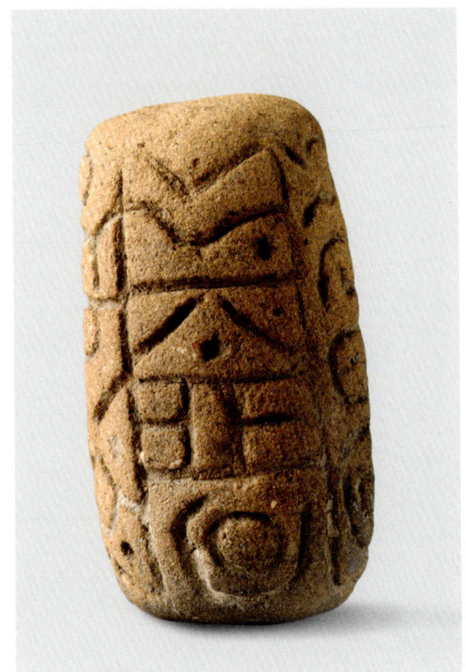

C 11

Culture: Coast of Manabì
(late Jama-Coaque)

Dimensions: 53 × 29

TLT: - 900 years

Object description:
cylindrical *sello* made of
brownish terracotta, not
axially perforated and
showing slightly convex
bases as well as slightly
rounded sides

Iconography: stylised face,
which can be read in either
direction, placed between
vertical displays of
geometric, spiral, tooth-
shaped patterns, etc.

Condition: partially worn off

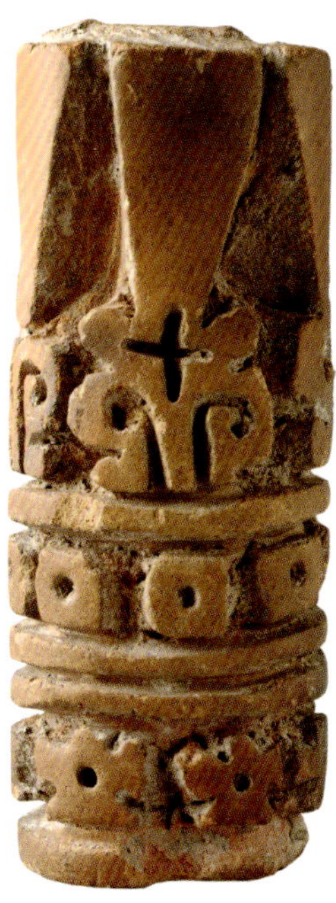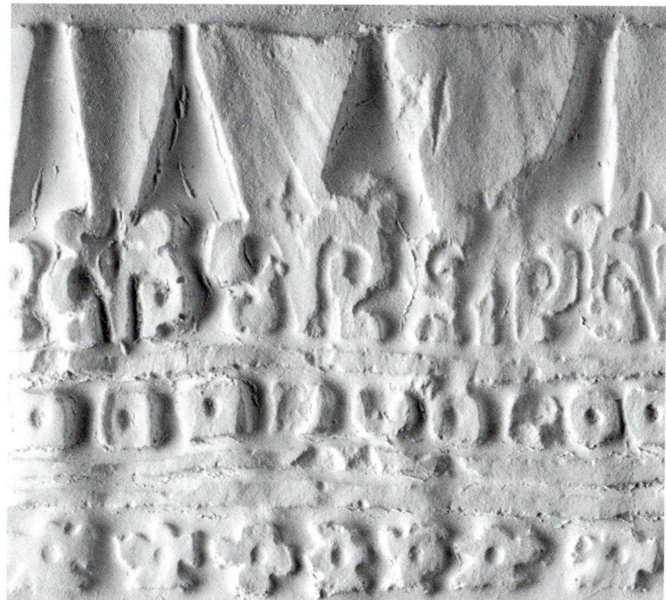

C 12

Culture: Jama-Coaque

Dimensions: 74 × 29

TLT: not available

Object description: cylindrical *sello* made of reddish-brown terracotta with concave bases, no axial perforation

Iconography: row of stylised masks (?) with ample head gear atop a series of ring-shaped bands interlaced with circle- (showing a central dot) and star-shaped patterns. At the bottom end a narrow circular indentation

Condition: the upper ring-shaped band is missing and there is a minor fracture in the lower one

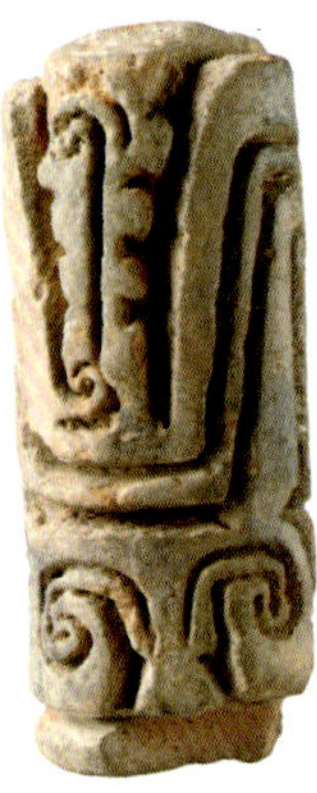

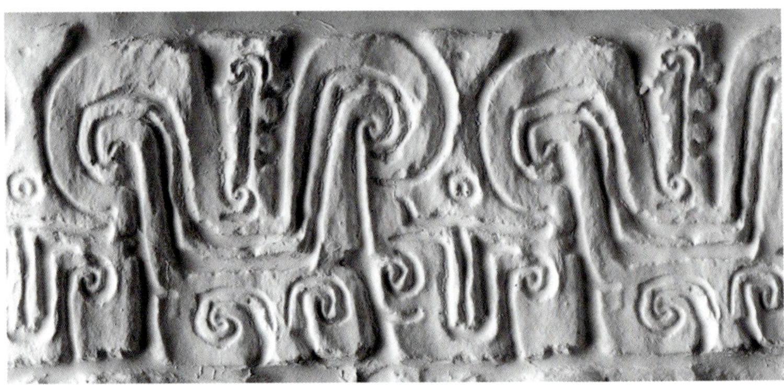

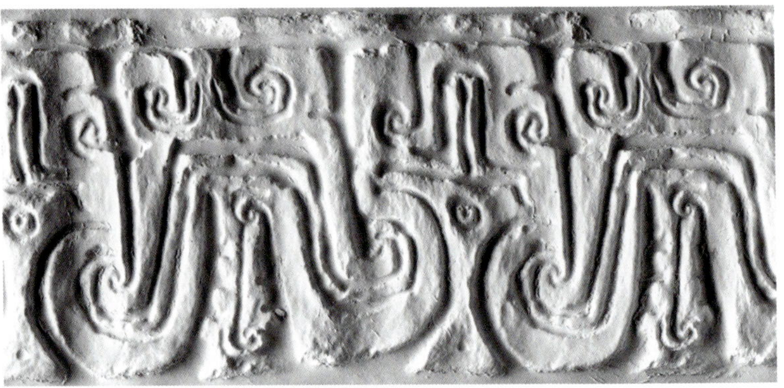

C 13

Culture: Coast of Manabì
(late Jama-Coaque)

Dimensions: 68 × 28

TLT: - 830 years

Object description:
cylindrical *sello* made of
brownish-grey terracotta, no
axial perforation and convex
butts

Iconography: row of stylised
masks with spiral-shaped
head gear (?). At both ends
two narrow circular
indentations

Condition: the ring-shaped
upper band is missing and
the lower one is partially
broken off

Culture: late Jama-Coaque

Dimensions: 55 × 25

TLT: - 1250 years

Object description:
cylindrical *sello* made of
brown-greyish terracotta,
no axial perforation, with
quadrilateral butts showing
concave sides flaring out at
the top

Iconography: two
superimposed tiers, each
consisting of a row of
isolated patterns showing a
double central S surrounded
by pennants (mask?). The
two tiers are offset against
each other

Condition: mostly intact, one
pattern partially broken off

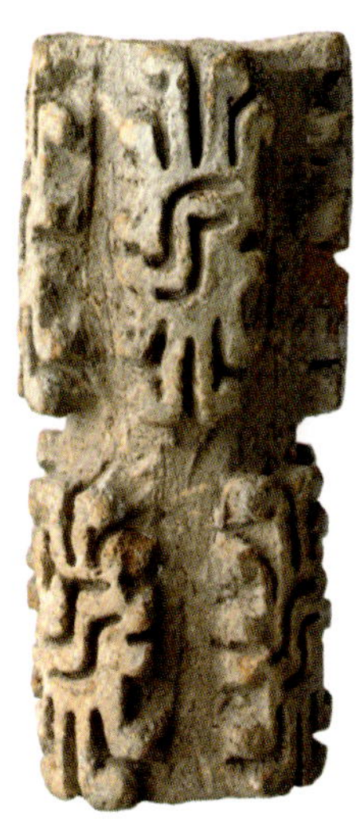
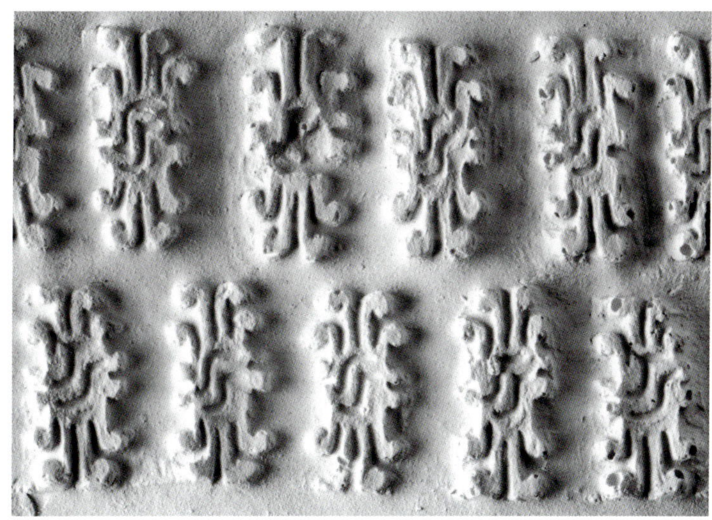

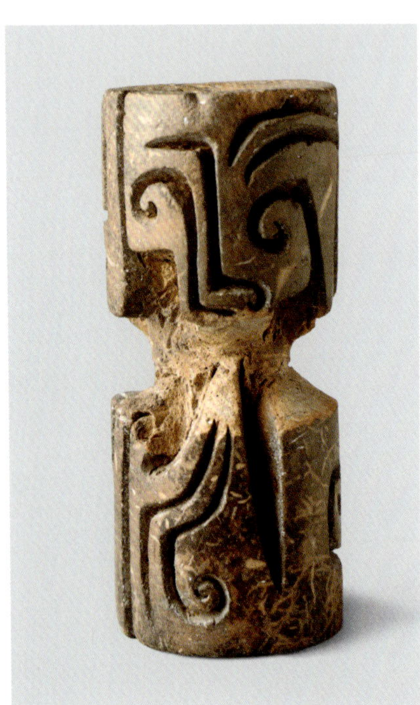

C 15

Culture: La Tolita

Dimensions: 62 × 28

TLT: - 1700 years

Object description: cylindrical *sello* made of brownish terracotta, no axial perforation

Iconography: various linear patterns ending in a spiral

Condition: deeply eroded in the median part on account of later grooving

Bibl. ref.: Estrada 1959: reproduced twice – by mistake – with numbers 144 and 150

C 16

Culture: Jama-Coaque

Dimensions: 77 × 32

TLT: - 1300 years

Object description: cylindrical *sello* made of brownish terracotta, axially perforated Ø 6

Iconography: two superimposed tiers with mirrored patterning – an indication of the bi-directionality of the *sello* – show twin figures holding hands. They are flanked by ape-like shape and linear as well as dotted patternings. At both ends linear and toothed bands

Condition: intact

Bibl. ref.: Cummins & Burgos 1996, p. 142, fig. 55a

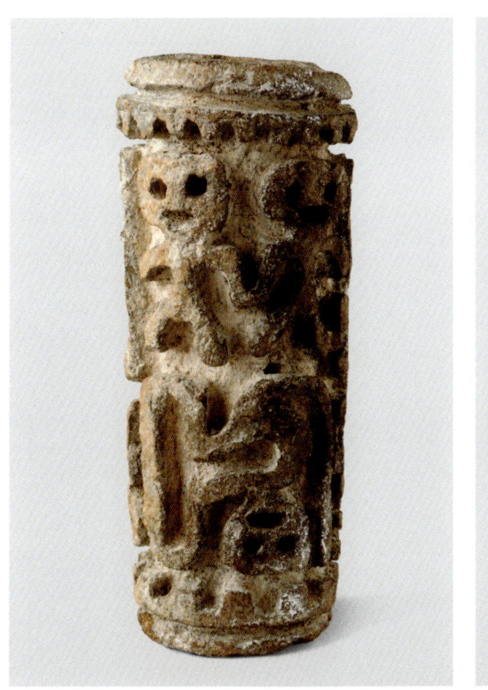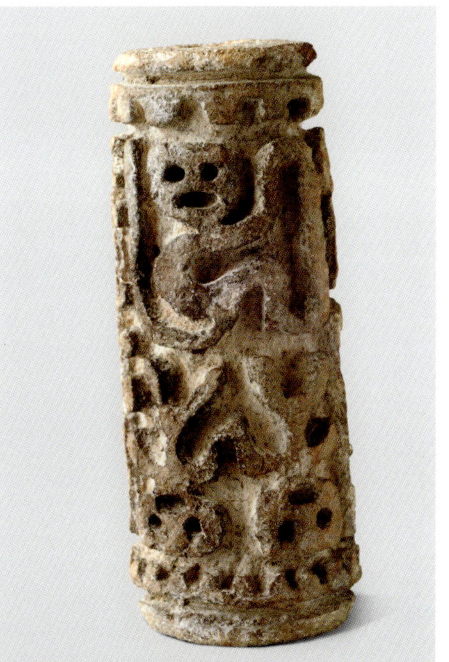

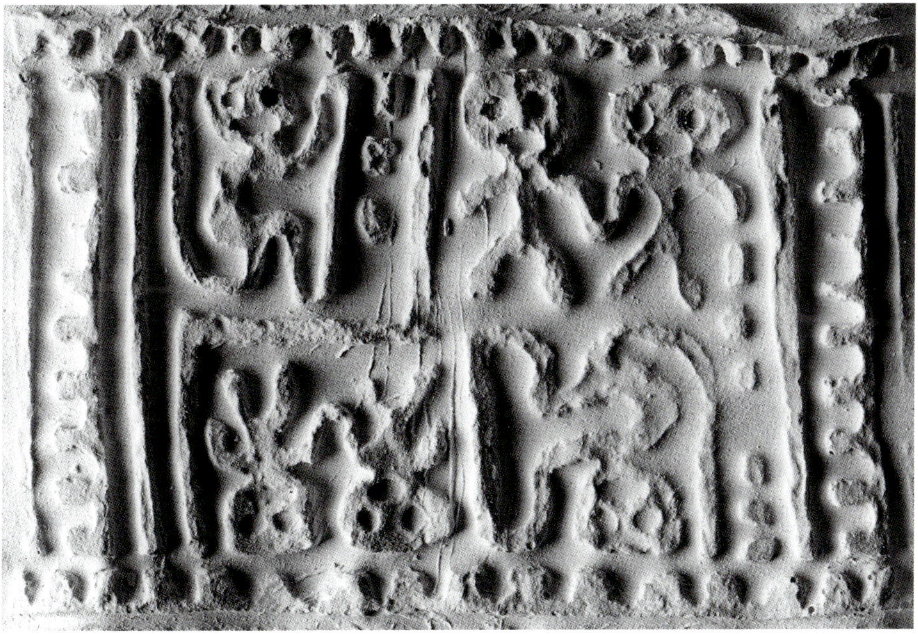

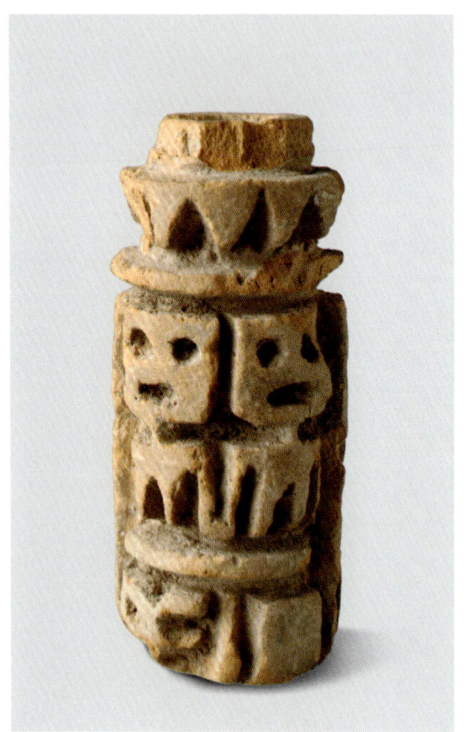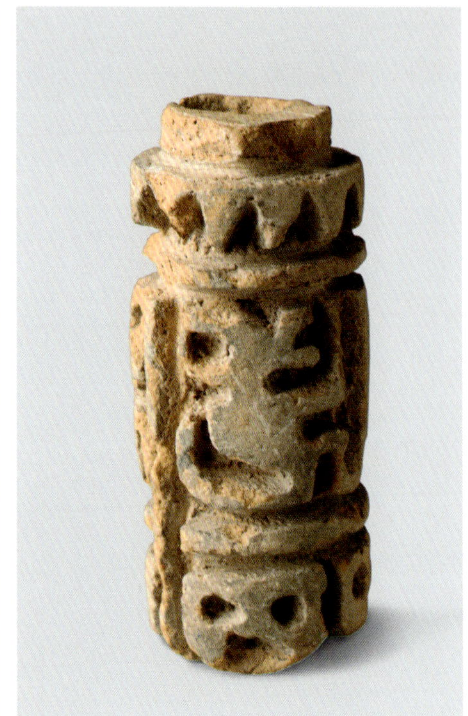

C 17

Culture: Jama-Coaque

Dimensions: 60 × 27

TLT: - 1600 years

Object description:
cylindrical *sello* made of
brownish terracotta, axially
perforated Ø 6. The ends
show traces of wear around
the hole

Iconography: two
superimposed tiers show
twin anthropomorphic
figures holding hands,
flanked by a zoomorphic
shape set between linear and
stairlike patterns. At each
end a toothed band set
between ring-shaped bands

Condition: lacks one end
piece

Bibl. ref.: Cummins &
Burgos 1996, p. 142, fig. 55a

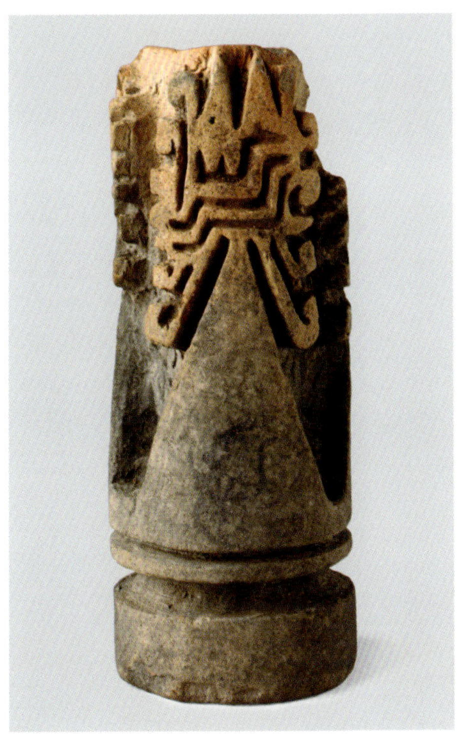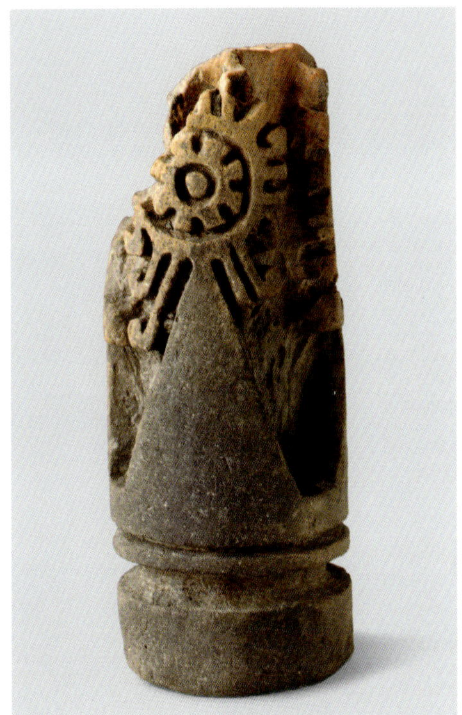

C 18

Culture: Jama-Coaque

Dimensions: 85 × 33

TLT: unavailable

Object description: cylindrical *sello* made of brown-greyish terracotta, axially perforated Ø 13. Ends show traces of wear around the hole

Iconography: twin stylised heads or masks (?) together with solar pattern set atop triangles and ring-shaped bands

Condition: the upper part is missing

Bibl. ref.: Cummins & Burgos 1996, p. 175, fig. 86a; p. 182, fig. 93b; p. 184, fig. 95b; p. 187, fig. 98a-b (all reproductions would seem to represent stylised plumed serpents)

123

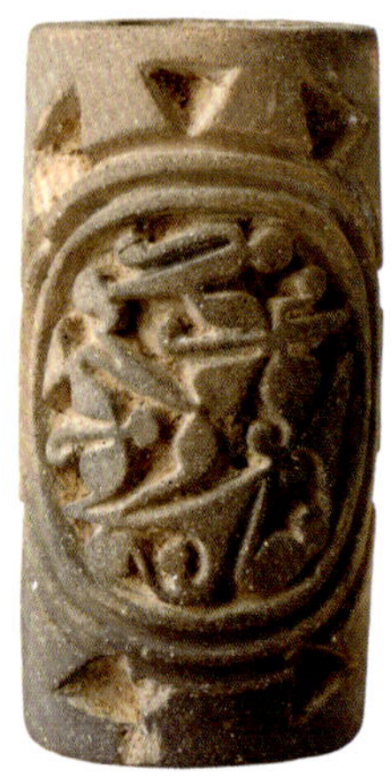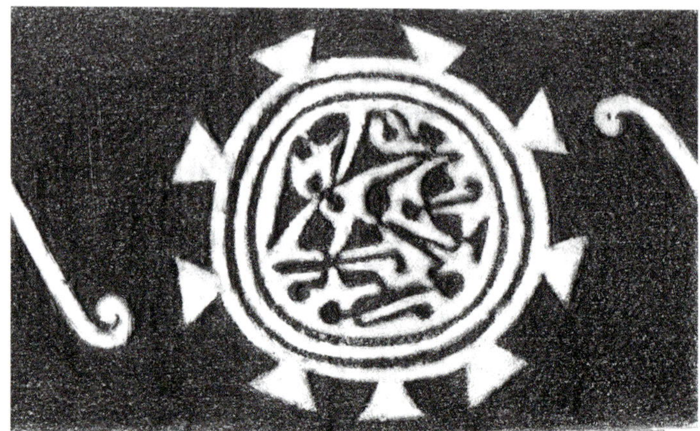

C 19

Culture: Jama-Coaque

Dimensions: 64.5 × 34

TLT: unavailable

Object description:
cylindrical *sello* made of
brownish terracotta with
greyish tones, axially
perforated Ø 17. Ends show
traces of wear around the
hole

Iconography: toothed
wheel containing a number
of figures, flanked by
S-shaped outline

Condition: intact

Bibl. ref.: Bodenhorst 1984,
fig. 22-A

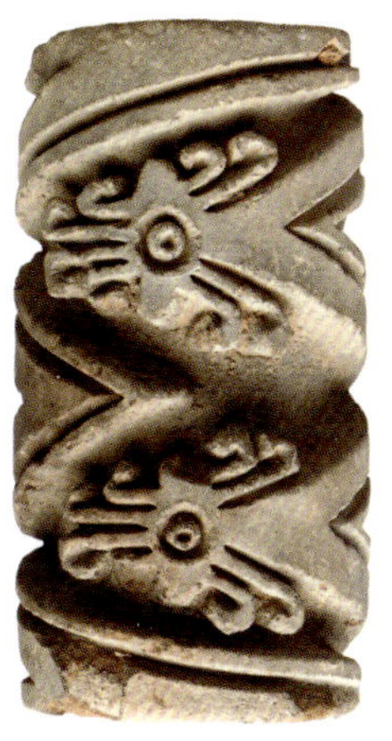 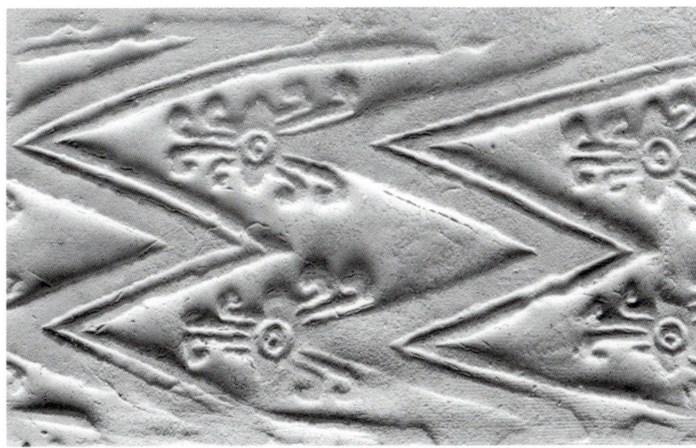

C 20

Culture: Jama-Coaque

Dimensions: 65 × 35

TLT: unavailable

Object description:
cylindrical *sello* made of
brownish terracotta, no axial
perforation. The butts are
concave

Iconography: V-shaped
bands segmented to acute
angle with trophy on the
cusp

Condition: intact

Bibl. ref.: Cummins &
Burgos 1996, group
'Stylisation of Fauna' own
section under the title
'The Plumed Serpent',
p. 196, fig. 107b, p. 197,
fig. 108a-b

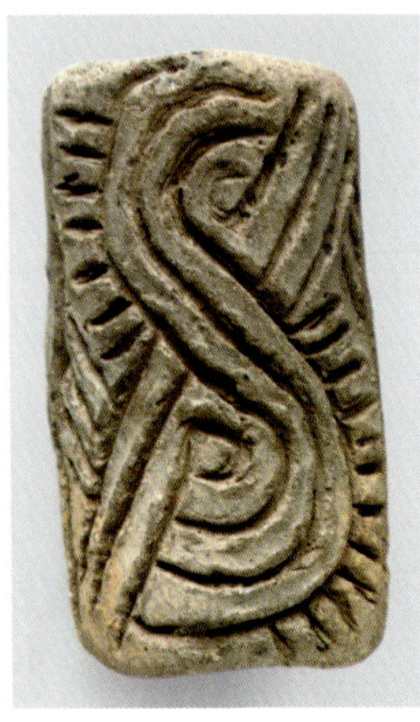 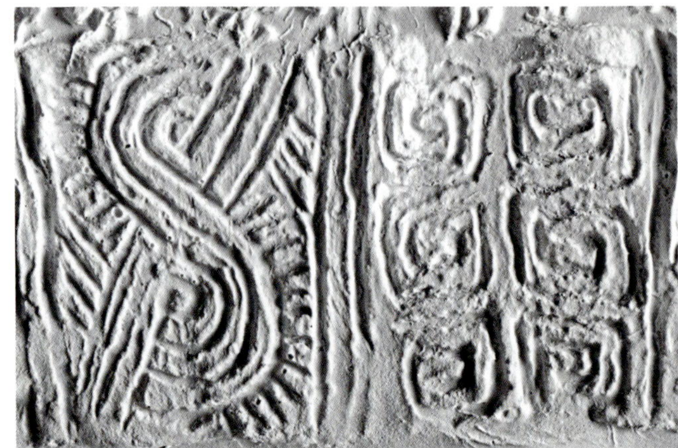

C 21

Culture: Manteña

Dimensions: 57 × 33

TLT: 630 years

Object description: brown terracotta cylindrical perforated – 16 mm

Iconography: S-shaped pattern (plumed serpent?)

Condition: intact

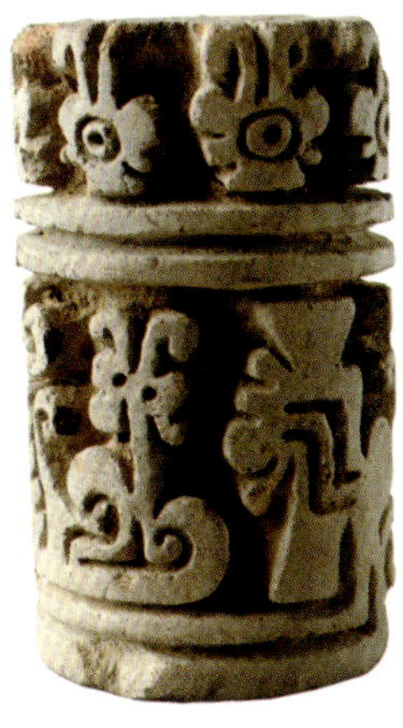 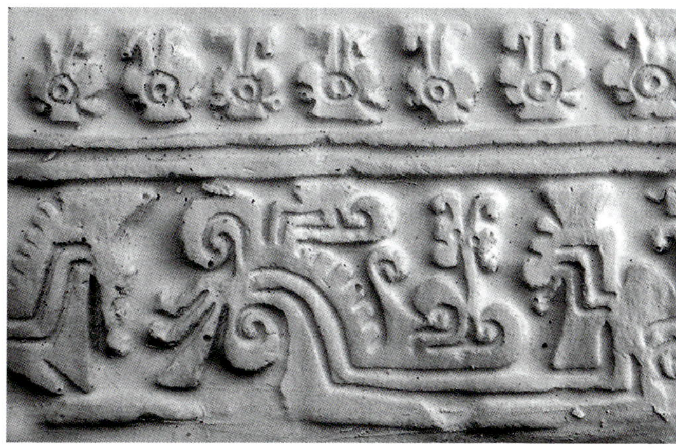

C 22

Culture: Jama-Coaque

Dimensions: 65 × 39

TLT: unavailable

Object description: brown terracotta cylindrical not perforated

Iconography: plumed serpent

Condition: intact

Bibl. ref.: Cummins & Burgos 1996, group 'Stylisation of Fauna' own section under the title 'The Plumed Serpent', p. 175, fig 86a, p. 176, fig. 87b, p. 182, fig. 93b